# Escape to Nature

## RV Camping Tips for National Park Enthusiasts

# Helen Taylor

# Table of Contents

# INTRODUCTION

Are you someone who has ever fantasized of getting away from the rush and bustle of everyday life, completely submerging yourself in the wild beauty of nature, and uncovering the hidden riches that are found in the national parks of the United States? If that is the case, you are not the only one. Considering that we live in a society that is saturated with devices, schedules, and stress, the allure of the great outdoors has never been more compelling.

The book "Escape to Nature: RV Camping Tips for National Park Enthusiasts" is the necessary guide you need to go on a transforming journey into the heart of some of the most breathtaking and awe-inspiring landscapes that our planet has to offer. It doesn't matter if you're an experienced RVer wishing to broaden your horizons or a newbie adventurer looking to experience the excitement of your first national park trip; this book is your key to unlocking the mysteries of RV camping in these natural wonders.

It is not just about traveling that the concept of RV camping in national parks is being discussed; rather, it is about escaping the mundane, reestablishing a connection with the natural world, and appreciating the enchantment of the great outdoors. Getting up to the sounds of birds singing, soaking in the warmth of a campfire, and looking up at a star-studded sky that is unaffected by the lights of the city are all aspects of this experience. Wildlife encounters, beautiful panoramas, and experiences that will last a lifetime are all part of the experience.

In this adventure, we will explore the delights and challenges of RV camping in national parks. We will share expert guidance, insider insights, and personal tales that will inspire and motivate you to embrace the wild, RV style of camping. Join us on this journey! Let's go on this journey together and explore the natural beauties that are waiting for us in the untouched playgrounds that our country has to offer. Welcome to "Escape to Nature."

# CHAPTER I

# Choosing the Right RV

## Types of RVs and their pros and cons

Recreational Vehicles (RVs) have become an increasingly popular way for people to explore the great outdoors while enjoying the comforts of home. As the RV market has expanded, various types of RVs have emerged to cater to different needs and preferences. Each type comes with its own set of pros and cons, making it crucial for potential buyers to understand their options before making a choice.

One of the most common types of RVs is the motorhome. Motorhomes are essentially self-contained homes on wheels, offering convenience and comfort for those who want to travel without towing a separate vehicle. This type has two primary categories: Class A and Class C motorhomes.

Class A motorhomes are the largest and most luxurious of the motorhome category. They often feature spacious living areas, full-size kitchens, and amenities like entertainment systems and slide-outs, which expand the living space when parked. Pros of Class A motorhomes include ample storage, high-end finishes, and the ability to accommodate large families or groups comfortably. However, their size can be a drawback, as they may be challenging to maneuver and park, and they tend to have lower fuel efficiency.

On the other hand, Class C motorhomes are smaller and more maneuverable than their Class A counterparts. They typically have a distinctive over-cab area that can be used for additional sleeping space or storage. Class C motorhomes balance comfort and convenience, making them a popular choice for families or couples looking for a more compact option. They are also typically more fuel-efficient but may have less interior space and fewer amenities compared to Class A models.

Travel trailers are another popular category of RVs, and they offer various sizes and layouts to suit different needs. These trailers are towed by a separate vehicle, such as a truck or SUV, making them a versatile choice for those who want to explore different destinations without needing a dedicated motorhome. Travel trailers can range from small teardrop trailers to large fifth-wheel trailers.

Teardrop trailers are the smallest and most lightweight option in the travel trailer category. They are easy to tow, making them suitable for smaller vehicles and first-time RVers. Teardrops usually feature a compact sleeping area and basic amenities like a small kitchenette. Their pros include affordability, easy towing, and efficient fuel usage. However, their compact size can be a drawback, as they may lack space and comfort for extended trips.

Conversely, fifth-wheel trailers are among the largest and most luxurious travel trailers available. They have a raised front section extending over the towing vehicle, providing additional living space and amenities. Fifth-wheels often feature multiple slide-outs, spacious kitchens, and full bathrooms, making them feel like a home away from home. Their pros include ample interior space, high-end features, and enhanced stability during towing due to their design. However, they require a specialized hitch in the bed of a pickup truck, limiting the types of vehicles that can tow them effectively.

Another category of RVs is camper vans, also known as Class B motorhomes. Camper vans are essentially converted vans that have been equipped with sleeping quarters, a small kitchen, and basic amenities. They are the smallest and most maneuverable type of motorhome, making them an ideal choice for solo travelers or couples seeking simplicity and ease of use. Camper vans are also versatile, allowing for both urban and wilderness exploration. Pros include compact size, good fuel efficiency, and navigating narrow roads and urban areas. However, they offer limited space and amenities compared to larger RVs.

Finally, there are truck campers, which are compact RVs that fit into the bed of a pickup truck. These campers are an excellent choice for those who want the flexibility to detach the camper and use their truck for other purposes. Truck campers come in various sizes and configurations, offering different comfort levels and amenities. Their pros include affordability, easy maneuverability, and the ability to tow other vehicles or trailers. However, their small size can be a drawback for travelers who desire more space and amenities.

In conclusion, the world of RVs offers a diverse range of options to cater to travelers' varied preferences and needs. Motorhomes, travel trailers, camper vans, and truck campers all come with their unique advantages and disadvantages. When choosing the right RV, it's essential to consider factors like size, budget, towing capacity, and desired amenities. By understanding the pros and cons of each type of RV, prospective buyers can make an informed decision and embark on their RV adventures with confidence, knowing they've chosen the vehicle that best suits their lifestyle and goals.

## Factors to consider when selecting an RV

Choosing the right recreational vehicle (RV) is a significant decision, whether you're a seasoned RVer looking to upgrade or a first-time buyer eager to embark on new adventures. With a wide array of RV types, sizes, and features on the market, selecting the perfect RV can be daunting. To make an informed choice, it's essential to consider several key factors that will shape your RV experience and ensure it aligns with your needs, preferences, and budget.

First and foremost, you should evaluate your budget and financial considerations. RVs come in various price points, from affordable entry-level models to high-end luxury options. Beyond the initial purchase price, you must factor in ongoing costs such as insurance, maintenance, campground fees, and fuel. It's crucial to establish a realistic budget that covers the RV's purchase and allows for comfortable and sustainable RV living without straining your finances.

Another vital consideration is the size and layout of the RV. RVs vary significantly in terms of their dimensions and interior layouts. The size of your RV should align with your travel plans, whether you intend to stay in campgrounds with full hookups or venture into more remote, off-grid locations. Larger RVs typically offer more space and amenities but can be challenging to maneuver and park, especially in tight spaces or in densely populated areas. Smaller RVs are easier to handle but may have limited living and storage space. Additionally, consider the interior layout to ensure it meets your specific needs and preferences, with features like a comfortable sleeping area, a functional kitchen, and adequate storage.

Weight and towing capacity are crucial considerations for travel trailer and fifth-wheel buyers. Your towing vehicle must be able to tow the RV you choose safely. It's essential to know your vehicle's towing limits and choose an RV that falls within them to ensure safety and performance while on the road. Remember that larger and heavier RVs may require a more substantial towing vehicle, which can impact your budget.

When selecting an RV, you should also consider the type of camping experience you desire. Are you planning on extended trips, full-time RV living, or occasional weekend getaways? Your intended use will influence your choice of RV. For frequent travelers or full-timers, a spacious, well-equipped RV with features like ample storage, a comfortable bedroom, and a well-appointed kitchen may be necessary. Weekend campers or those who prioritize mobility and simplicity may opt for smaller, more compact RVs that are easier to set up and pack down.

It's crucial to consider the seasonality of your RV adventures. If you plan to use your RV year-round or in various weather conditions, you'll want to ensure it is appropriately equipped for all seasons. Some RVs have features like insulation, dual-pane windows, and heated tanks, making them suitable for cold-weather camping. Conversely, if you primarily camp in warm climates, you might prioritize features like air conditioning and ventilation. Be sure to select an RV that matches your preferred travel destinations and seasons.

Maintenance and repair considerations should not be overlooked. RVs, like any vehicle or home, require regular maintenance to maintain good working conditions. Some RVs may be more complex and require specialized maintenance, while others are simpler and easier to maintain. Consider your mechanical aptitude and willingness to perform maintenance tasks or whether you plan to rely on professional RV service providers. Ease of maintenance can save you time, money, and stress over the life of your RV.

Furthermore, it's essential to contemplate your lifestyle and preferences when selecting an RV. Are you a minimalist who values simplicity and the freedom to travel lightly, or do you prefer the comforts of a fully equipped home on wheels? Some RVs are designed for off-grid living, offering solar panels, composting toilets, and water purification systems, while others cater to those who prefer the convenience of full hookups and campground amenities. Understanding your preferred lifestyle will help you choose an RV that enhances your overall experience on the road.

The RV manufacturers' and dealerships' reputations and reliability are also critical factors to consider. Research and read reviews to ensure that your chosen brand has a history of producing quality RVs and providing excellent customer service. Additionally, buying from a reputable dealership with a strong track record of customer satisfaction and after-sales support is advisable.

Lastly, think about the long-term perspective. Are you purchasing an RV for short-term adventures, or do you envision yourself enjoying the RV lifestyle for many years to come? RV depreciation can vary significantly, so consider how well your chosen RV will hold its value over time. Some brands and models retain their value better than others, which can be an essential factor if you plan to sell or trade in your RV in the future.

In conclusion, selecting the right RV is a decision that requires careful consideration of various factors, including budget, size, layout, towing capacity, intended use, seasonal requirements, maintenance, lifestyle preferences, manufacturer reputation, and long-term value. By thoroughly assessing these factors and conducting thorough research, you can make an informed choice that aligns with your unique needs and ensures a fulfilling and enjoyable RVing experience. Whether you're a weekend warrior or a full-time traveler, the perfect RV is out there, waiting to take you on your next adventure.

## Budget considerations and buying tips

Purchasing a recreational vehicle (RV) is a significant investment, one that offers the promise of adventure and freedom on the open road. However, navigating the budget considerations and making informed buying decisions are essential steps in the RV ownership journey. This section will explore various budget considerations and provide valuable buying tips to help you make a well-informed decision when selecting the RV that best suits your needs, preferences, and financial capabilities.

Establishing a realistic budget is one of the first budget considerations when buying an RV. An RV purchase involves not only the initial cost but also ongoing expenses such as insurance, maintenance, fuel, campground fees, and the cost of outfitting your RV with necessary accessories and supplies. Begin by assessing your financial situation and determining how much you can comfortably allocate to your RV adventure. Be honest with yourself about what you can afford, and avoid overextending your finances, as this can lead to stress and financial strain down the road.

Once you've determined your budget, exploring your financing options is crucial. RV financing can be obtained through banks, credit unions, RV dealerships, or specialized RV lenders. Compare interest rates, terms, and loan conditions to find the most favorable financing option that aligns with your budget. Consider making a substantial down payment if possible, as this can lower your monthly payments and overall interest costs.

Another critical budget consideration is the type of RV you choose. RVs come in various sizes, classes, and price points. Class A motorhomes and larger travel trailers tend to be more expensive, while smaller Class B motorhomes, teardrop trailers, and camper vans are typically more budget-friendly. Remember that larger RVs may come with higher operating costs, including fuel consumption and campground fees. Assess your budget and travel needs carefully to strike a balance between the size and features of your RV and your financial capabilities.

In addition to the purchase price, buyers must also account for taxes and registration fees when budgeting for their RV. These costs can vary significantly by location, so it's advisable to research the specific requirements in your state or region to avoid unexpected expenses. Additionally, some states may impose annual taxes or fees on RV ownership, so be prepared for ongoing costs associated with ownership.

When buying an RV, it's essential to consider the insurance cost. RV insurance is a specialized type of coverage that considers the unique features and uses of recreational vehicles. Factors that influence the cost of insurance include the type and size of the RV, your driving history, the level of coverage you choose, and your location. Obtaining insurance quotes from multiple providers is advisable to find the most competitive rates while ensuring that your chosen coverage adequately protects your investment.

Maintenance and repairs are ongoing expenses that should not be overlooked. Like any vehicle or home, RVs require regular maintenance to remain safe and functional. Maintenance costs can vary widely depending on the type of RV and how often you use it. Larger, more complex RVs may require more extensive and costly maintenance, while smaller and simpler models tend to have lower maintenance costs. It's essential to budget for routine maintenance tasks, as well as unexpected repairs that can arise during your travels.

One budget-saving tip is to learn how to perform basic maintenance tasks yourself. Routine tasks such as oil changes, tire checks, and minor repairs can be done by RV owners with some knowledge and the right tools. By taking a hands-on approach to maintenance, you can reduce labor costs and better understand your RV's mechanics.

Campground fees can be a significant part of your RVing budget, especially if you plan to stay in private campgrounds or RV resorts. These fees can vary widely based on location, amenities, and time of year. Some campgrounds offer discounts for longer stays or memberships in camping clubs, which can help reduce your overall camping expenses. Additionally, consider exploring free or low-cost camping options, such as national forests, Bureau of Land Management (BLM) lands, and state parks, to stretch your budget further.

When buying an RV, one of the most crucial tips is to thoroughly research and inspect the unit before making a purchase. Start by researching different RV brands, models, and floorplans to determine which suits your needs best. Pay attention to user reviews and ratings to gain insights into the quality and reliability of specific RVs. Once you've identified a potential RV, conduct a thorough inspection. If buying new, carefully review the manufacturer's warranty and any extended warranty options. For used RVs, hire a qualified RV inspector to assess the unit's condition, including the chassis, engine, appliances, plumbing, and electrical systems. An inspection can uncover hidden issues that may not be apparent to the untrained eye and help you avoid costly repairs down the road.

When negotiating the purchase price of your RV, don't hesitate to negotiate with the seller or dealership. Be prepared to walk away if the price doesn't align with your budget or expectations. Requesting a detailed history of the RV's maintenance and service records is also advisable, as this can provide valuable insights into its care and potential issues.

Consider the cost of outfitting your RV with essential accessories and supplies. Items like kitchen equipment, bedding, camping gear, and safety equipment should be factored into your budget. Look for deals and discounts when shopping for these items to minimize your overall expenses.

Lastly, plan for unexpected expenses and emergencies when budgeting for your RV adventure. An emergency fund can provide peace of mind and financial security in case of unexpected repairs, medical emergencies, or other unforeseen challenges during your travels.

In conclusion, selecting and purchasing an RV involves carefully assessing your budget and financial capabilities. Establish a realistic budget, explore financing options, and consider the ongoing expenses associated with RV ownership, including taxes, insurance, maintenance, and campground fees. Thoroughly research RV options, inspect units, negotiate prices, and factor in the cost of essential accessories and supplies. By taking these budget considerations and buying tips into account, you can confidently embark on your RV journey, knowing that you've made a well-informed decision that aligns with your financial goals and travel aspirations.

# CHAPTER II

# Planning Your National Park Adventure

## Researching and selecting national parks

The allure of the great outdoors and the world's natural wonders draw countless adventurers and nature enthusiasts to national parks each year. From Yellowstone's iconic grandeur to Acadia's serene beauty, the United States is home to a vast and diverse collection of national parks, each offering a unique and awe-inspiring experience. However, with so many options available, researching and selecting the right national parks for your adventure is crucial in ensuring a fulfilling and memorable journey.

One of the first considerations when researching national parks is your specific interests and preferences. Do you crave the sight of majestic mountains, pristine lakes, lush forests, or expansive deserts? Are you a wildlife enthusiast, a hiker, a photographer, or simply someone seeking solitude and tranquility in nature? Identifying your interests and preferences will help narrow down the list of national parks that align with your goals, ensuring you choose destinations that resonate with your passions.

Geography plays a significant role in your selection process. National parks are spread across the United States, encompassing various ecosystems and climates. Some parks are located in the Pacific Northwest, offering lush rainforests and coastal beauty, while others are nestled in the Southwest, showcasing rugged deserts and iconic rock formations. Research the geographical regions that appeal to you and consider the climate and weather conditions during your planned visit to select parks that align with your comfort level.

Once you've identified your interests and preferred geographic regions, delve into the individual national parks to gather more detailed information. The National Park Service website (nps.gov) is an invaluable resource, offering comprehensive information on each park, including park maps, visitor center locations, and details on park amenities and activities. It's also an excellent source for checking current park conditions, road closures, and entrance fees.

In addition to the official National Park Service website, numerous guidebooks, travel blogs, and online forums provide insights and recommendations from fellow travelers. Reading about the experiences of others who have visited the parks you're interested in can offer valuable insights and tips for planning your own adventure. These resources often include personal anecdotes, photographs, and detailed descriptions of hikes and points of interest.

Beyond the online realm, don't hesitate to visit your local library or bookstore to browse travel guides and books dedicated to national parks. These publications often provide in-depth information about park history, geology, flora, fauna, and recreational opportunities. They can serve as comprehensive references as you plan your visit and explore the park's natural and cultural significance.

Consider the time of year you plan to visit the national parks, which can significantly impact your experience. Many parks have distinct seasons, each offering its own set of activities and attractions. Summer may be ideal for hiking and camping, while autumn showcases vibrant foliage, and winter invites opportunities for snowshoeing and cross-country skiing. Timing your visit to align with your interests and the park's seasonal highlights can enhance your experience and provide unique perspectives.

Accessibility is another critical factor to consider when selecting national parks. Some parks are easily accessible by car and offer a range of visitor services, including campgrounds, lodges, and restaurants. Others may require more extensive planning and travel, involving backcountry camping and remote hiking. Ensure that your chosen parks align with your desired level of accessibility and the type of adventure you're seeking.

When planning your national park adventure, it's essential to consider your fitness level and outdoor experience. National parks offer various recreational activities, from leisurely nature walks to strenuous backpacking trips. Assess your physical capabilities and comfort in outdoor settings to choose parks and activities that match your fitness level. Additionally, if you're considering more challenging activities, such as backcountry camping or mountaineering, ensure you have the necessary skills, equipment, and permits.

Budget considerations also play a significant role in the selection process. The cost of visiting national parks can vary widely, depending on entrance fees, campground fees, and accommodation options. Some parks offer annual passes that provide access to multiple parks for a single fee, while others require separate entrance fees for each visit. Research the fees and costs associated with your chosen parks to create a realistic budget for your adventure.

Environmental awareness and responsible travel are essential when visiting national parks. Familiarize yourself with Leave No Trace principles, which emphasize responsible outdoor ethics to minimize your impact on the environment. Respect park regulations, stay on designated trails, and avoid disturbing wildlife. By practicing eco-friendly and ethical behavior, you contribute to preserving these natural treasures for future generations.

Finally, consider the level of crowds and popularity when selecting national parks. Iconic parks like Yellowstone and Yosemite can become crowded during peak seasons, leading to limited availability for campsites and parking. If you prefer a quieter and more intimate experience, explore less-visited parks and consider visiting during the shoulder seasons or weekdays to avoid the crowds.

In conclusion, researching and selecting national parks for your outdoor adventure is a thoughtful and rewarding process. Begin by identifying your interests, geographic preferences, and specific activities you'd like to pursue. Utilize online resources, travel guides, and personal recommendations to gather information about each park's unique features and offerings. Consider the season, accessibility, fitness level, budget, and environmental responsibility when choosing. By carefully planning and selecting national parks that align with your interests and values, you can embark on a journey of discovery, connection with nature, and unforgettable experiences in some of the most breathtaking landscapes our nation offers.


## Setting a travel itinerary

Embarking on an RV adventure is a dream for many, offering the freedom to explore the open road, discover new landscapes, and create lasting memories. However, to make the most of your journey, it's essential to set a travel itinerary that aligns with your interests, time frame, and the unique features of your RV. In this section, we'll explore the key considerations and steps involved in crafting a well-planned travel itinerary for your RV adventure.

The first and foremost step in setting a travel itinerary is defining your travel goals and objectives. What do you hope to achieve during your RV adventure? Are you seeking relaxation and leisure, outdoor adventures, cultural exploration, or a combination of these experiences? Identifying your travel goals will help shape your itinerary and guide your decision-making process as you plan your route and activities.

Next, consider the duration of your RV trip. Whether you're planning a weekend getaway, a month-long expedition, or a full-time RV lifestyle, the length of your journey will significantly influence your itinerary. Shorter trips may focus on a specific region or theme, while longer journeys offer the flexibility to explore a broader range of destinations.

One of the most exciting aspects of RV travel is the freedom to choose your destinations. National parks, scenic byways, coastal routes, and historic sites are just a few of the options available to RV enthusiasts. Research the destinations that pique your interest and align with your travel goals. Consider factors such as the distance between stops, the availability of RV-friendly campgrounds, and the activities and attractions in each area.

It's important to balance planning and spontaneity when crafting your travel itinerary. While having a general outline of your route and destinations is essential, leave room for flexibility and unexpected discoveries. RV travel often leads to unforeseen detours and unplanned stops, so embrace the freedom to adapt your itinerary as you go.

Consider the pace of your journey. Some travelers prefer a leisurely pace, spending several days or even weeks at each destination, while others opt for a faster-paced itinerary with shorter stays. Your travel style should align with your interests and energy levels. A slower pace may be ideal if you enjoy deep exploration and immersion in local culture. On the other hand, if you have a desire to cover more ground and experience a variety of locations, a faster pace may be more suitable.

Researching and planning for the practical aspects of your RV adventure is essential. Identify RV campgrounds or overnight parking options at each destination in advance, especially during peak travel seasons when campgrounds can fill up quickly. Ensure that the campgrounds you choose offer the amenities and facilities you require, such as hookups, dump stations, and recreational activities.

Mapping out your route is a critical step in setting a travel itinerary. Utilize navigation apps, GPS devices, or traditional paper maps to plan your route and estimate driving times between destinations. Keep in mind that RV travel often involves slower driving speeds and consideration for the size and height of your RV, so plan your daily distances accordingly.

While planning your route, consider the scenic byways and off-the-beaten-path routes that can add a touch of adventure and discovery to your journey. These routes often lead to hidden gems, picturesque landscapes, and unique cultural experiences that may not be accessible via major highways.

Another essential aspect of setting a travel itinerary is managing your travel budget. RV travel expenses include fuel, campground fees, food, activities, and miscellaneous costs. Develop a daily or weekly budget that outlines your expected expenses and ensures that you stay within your financial limits. Be prepared for unexpected expenses or emergencies by setting aside a contingency fund.

Factor in downtime and relaxation into your itinerary. RV travel can be exhilarating, but it can also be physically demanding. Schedule rest days or leisurely afternoons to recharge, relax, and enjoy the simple pleasures of RV living, such as a campfire, a book by the campsite, or a peaceful walk in nature.

Embrace the spirit of adventure by exploring local cuisine, culture, and attractions at each destination. Seek out local restaurants, markets, and festivals to savor regional flavors and experiences. Engage with local communities to gain insights into the area's history, traditions, and way of life. Whether it's tasting regional specialties or participating in local events, immersing yourself in the culture of each destination can enrich your RV adventure.

Safety is paramount when setting a travel itinerary. Familiarize yourself with road conditions, weather forecasts, and potential hazards along your route. Check your RV's condition, including tires, brakes, and all systems, before hitting the road. Share your itinerary and travel plans with a trusted friend or family member, and establish a communication plan in case of emergencies. As

you embark on your RV adventure, keep a travel journal or blog to document your experiences, impressions, and memories. Capturing your journey in writing, photographs, or videos allows you to relive the moments and share your adventures with others. It also serves as a valuable resource for future trips and a way to preserve the legacy of your RV travels.

In conclusion, setting a travel itinerary for your RV adventure is essential in maximizing your enjoyment and fulfillment on the road. Define your travel goals, consider the duration of your journey, and choose destinations that align with your interests and preferences. Strike a balance between planning and spontaneity, and be prepared to adapt your itinerary as you go. Plan your route, research campgrounds, manage your budget, and prioritize safety. Embrace the opportunities for discovery and cultural immersion, and don't forget to document your journey for future reflection and inspiration. With a well-crafted travel itinerary, your RV adventure can become a transformative and unforgettable experience that takes you to the heart of nature, culture, and adventure.

## Reserving campsites and permits

Embarking on an RV trip is an exciting adventure, offering the opportunity to explore the beauty of nature and the freedom of the open road. To make the most of your journey, it's crucial to plan and secure your accommodations in advance by reserving campsites and obtaining any necessary permits. This section will explore the key considerations and steps involved in reserving campsites and permits for your RV trip.

One of the first considerations when planning your RV trip is choosing the destinations and campgrounds you want to visit. Research national parks, state parks, campgrounds, and RV parks in the areas you plan to explore. Determine the availability of campgrounds that can accommodate RVs, considering factors such as campground amenities, proximity to points of interest, and the availability of full hookups, if desired.

After identifying your preferred campgrounds, it's time to check their availability and make reservations. Reservations are particularly crucial during peak travel seasons and popular destinations, as campgrounds can fill up quickly. Many campgrounds, especially those within national and state parks, offer online reservation systems that allow you to check availability and book your campsite well in advance. To secure your desired dates and locations, it's advisable to make reservations as early as possible, sometimes up to a year in advance for high-demand sites.

When making reservations for your RV trip, be prepared with the necessary information, including the dates of your stay, the size and type of your RV, and any specific campground preferences. Some campgrounds have restrictions on RV length, so ensure that your RV fits within the designated site size limits. Additionally, confirm that the selected campground can accommodate your needs if you require full water, electricity, and sewage hookups.

Consider the duration of your stay at each campground when making reservations. Some travelers prefer shorter stays, while others may opt for more extended visits to explore the area thoroughly. Be mindful of the campgrounds' maximum stay limits, as these can vary by location and may affect your travel plans.
Flexibility can enhance your RV trip experience, so consider mixing reservations with spontaneous stops along the way. While making advance reservations ensures you have a place to stay at your chosen destinations, leaving room for flexibility allows you to adapt your itinerary based on your interests, weather conditions, and unexpected discoveries.

Stay informed about campground rules and regulations during your RV trip. Familiarize yourself with check-in and check-out times, quiet hours, waste disposal guidelines, and any specific rules related to campfires or generator use. Respecting campground rules ensures a harmonious experience for all campers and helps protect the environment and maintain the beauty of the natural surroundings.
In addition to reserving campsites, some RV trips may require permits for specific activities or locations. For example, you may need permits if you plan to camp in national parks' backcountry areas, hike on wilderness trails, or engage in activities such as fishing or boating. Research the permit requirements for your chosen destinations and activities well in advance to ensure compliance with regulations.

Obtaining permits often involves an application process, fees, and specific guidelines for responsible outdoor recreation. It's essential to apply for permits early, as some permits are limited in quantity and may be in high demand. Review the application deadlines, fees, and any required documentation or certifications to complete the permit process successfully.

National parks, in particular, have various permit requirements and fees for recreational activities such as hiking, camping, and backcountry exploration. These permits are designed to manage visitor use, protect sensitive ecosystems, and ensure the safety of outdoor enthusiasts. Some permits can be obtained online, while others may require in-person registration at visitor centers or ranger stations.

Check the specific regulations for RV trips that include boating or fishing for each location. Some bodies of water may have restrictions on boat size, motor type, and fishing seasons. Ensure you have the licenses, permits, and equipment to enjoy these activities responsibly and legally.

In addition to permits for specific activities, certain RV trips may require entrance or park passes, depending on the locations you plan to visit. National parks, state parks, and other public lands often charge entrance fees to fund park maintenance and conservation efforts. Purchasing an annual park pass or an interagency pass can save costs if you visit multiple parks and recreation areas during your RV trip.

Finally, when making reservations and obtaining permits for your RV trip, keep a record of all confirmations, reservation numbers, permit documents, and contact information for the campgrounds and park offices. Having this information readily available can be helpful in case of any questions or issues during your journey.

In conclusion, reserving campsites and obtaining permits for an RV trip are crucial aspects of trip planning that can enhance your overall experience. Begin by researching and selecting campgrounds that align with your travel goals, RV size, and preferences. Make advance reservations for your preferred campgrounds to secure your accommodations, especially during peak seasons. Be prepared with the necessary information when making reservations and ensure compliance with campground rules and regulations during your stay.

Conduct thorough research and apply for permits for activities and locations that require permits well before your trip. Familiarize yourself with the specific requirements, deadlines, and fees associated with permits and park passes. By proactively addressing these aspects of your RV trip planning, you can ensure a smooth and enjoyable journey filled with memorable experiences in the natural beauty of your chosen destinations.

## Preparing for different seasons and weather conditions

Embarking on a recreational vehicle (RV) trip presents a unique set of challenges and delights, with the variability of seasons and weather conditions playing a pivotal role in shaping the experience. Unlike traditional travel, where accommodations often provide a stable, climate-controlled environment, RV travelers are more directly exposed to the whims of nature. This section delves into the essential considerations and preparations one must undertake to ensure a safe and enjoyable RV trip across different seasons and weather conditions.

The allure of an RV trip lies in its flexibility and the close connection it offers with the outdoors. However, this intimacy with nature demands a thorough understanding and respect for the elements. Preparation is key, and it begins with a comprehensive understanding of the seasonal weather patterns of your destinations. Researching historical weather data, staying updated with current forecasts, and understanding regional climatic variations are crucial steps. This knowledge influences your packing list and informs your route planning and timing.

Spring and autumn present a particularly challenging scenario due to their transitional nature. These seasons often bring unpredictable weather, with the possibility of sudden temperature shifts, rain, and late or early snowfall in some regions. Preparing for a wide range of temperatures is vital for spring journeys. Layered clothing is essential, allowing for easy adaptation to changing conditions. Waterproof gear and a reliable heating system in your RV are necessary to handle rain and chilly nights. In contrast, autumn trips may require additional warmth as temperatures drop, particularly in the evenings. Heavier bedding, extra blankets, and appropriate attire for cooler weather are indispensable.

With its generally warmer and more stable weather, summer might seem like the ideal season for RV travel. However, it comes with its own set of challenges, such as extreme heat and sudden thunderstorms. Ensuring your RV's air conditioning system is in top condition is crucial. Sunshades, awnings, and breathable, light-colored clothing help manage the heat. Moreover, preparing for rain and potential storms involves securing a weatherproof canopy, having a stock of sandbags or weights for stabilization, and understanding the safety protocols in case of severe weather.

Winter RV travel, though less common, offers a serene and unique experience. However, it demands the most rigorous preparations. The primary concern is the cold. Ensuring your RV's insulation is up to par, having a reliable heating system, and protecting water lines from freezing are vital steps. Snow and ice present additional hazards. Equipping your RV with snow tires, carrying chains, and understanding snow driving techniques are essential for safety. Moreover, packing emergency supplies such as extra food, water, blankets, and a well-equipped first-aid kit is crucial in case of unexpected severe weather conditions.

Regardless of the season, there are several universal preparations. First, a well-maintained RV is essential for any trip. Regular engine, brakes, tires, and batteries checks are critical for ensuring a safe journey. Second, an emergency kit tailored to the season and potential weather conditions is a must-have. This kit should include first-aid, tools, extra batteries, flashlights, and appropriate emergency food and water supplies. Third, staying informed is crucial. Access to real-time weather updates and understanding the local emergency protocols can significantly impact responding to unexpected weather changes.

In addition to these physical preparations, mental readiness is equally important. Weather can be unpredictable, and flexibility is a key trait for any RV traveler. Being prepared to alter routes, adjust schedules, or even cut a trip short due to unforeseen weather conditions is part of the journey. This flexibility, coupled with a well-prepared RV and a thorough understanding of the possible challenges, ensures the journey remains enjoyable and safe.

Finally, it's important to remember that each season offers its unique beauty and opportunities. Spring brings blooming landscapes, summer offers extended daylight for exploration, autumn dazzles with its colorful foliage, and winter presents a quiet, pristine world. Embracing the distinctiveness of each season and preparing accordingly allows RV travelers to experience and appreciate the diverse tapestry of nature fully.

In conclusion, preparing for an RV trip's different seasons and weather conditions requires a multi-faceted approach, encompassing thorough research, meticulous planning, and a flexible mindset. The rewards of such preparation are immense, offering a safe and profoundly enriching travel experience that brings one closer to the rhythms of nature. Whether braving the unpredictability of spring, basking in the summer sun, reveling in autumn's colors, or navigating a winter wonderland, an RV trip can be a profoundly memorable journey with the right preparations.

# CHAPTER III

# RV Essentials

## Packing checklist for RV camping

Embarking on an RV camping adventure is an exciting endeavor, blending a home's comforts with the thrill of the great outdoors. However, the success of such a trip largely hinges on thorough preparation and packing. Unlike traditional camping, RV camping offers the luxury of space and facilities, but it also demands a more comprehensive checklist to ensure you have all the essentials for both the journey and the destination. This section aims to provide an in-depth guide to packing for an RV camping trip, ensuring that travelers are well- equipped for a seamless and enjoyable experience.

First and foremost, the cornerstone of RV camping is the vehicle itself. Ensuring that the RV is in top condition should be the primary task. This includes thoroughly checking the engine, brakes, tires, and batteries. Additionally, it is essential to ensure that all the RV utilities are functioning correctly. This includes the gas, water, and electrical systems. A well-maintained RV guarantees safety on the road and ensures comfort during the camping.

Once the RV's readiness is assured, attention must turn to the essentials of living. One of the biggest advantages of RV camping is the ability to cook and store food. Packing a well-thought-out assortment of non-perishable food items and ingredients for meals is essential. Canned goods, pasta, rice, and snacks are staples. Planning meals around these opportunities is a good idea if the trip includes stops at places where fresh produce is available. Equally important is ensuring the RV is equipped with cooking essentials: pots, pans, utensils, dish soap, and necessary appliances like a portable grill or a slow cooker.

Clothing is another critical aspect. The key here is to pack for the weather, considering the destination's climate and the season. Layered clothing is advisable for most camping trips as it offers flexibility for varying temperatures. Don't forget rain gear, sturdy footwear for hiking, and comfortable shoes for lounging around the campsite. Considering the limited laundry facilities, it's also important to pack enough clothes for the duration of the trip.

Sleeping arrangements are an integral part of RV camping. While RVs offer the comfort of a bed, ensuring you have appropriate bedding is crucial. This includes sheets, blankets, pillows, and sleeping bags if the weather is colder. Packaging extra tents, sleeping bags, and air mattresses is a good idea for additional guests or if you plan to spend any time tent camping.

Next, attention must be given to the tools and equipment necessary for a smooth camping experience. This includes a toolkit with basic tools like screwdrivers, pliers, a hammer, and a multi-tool. Including RV-specific items like leveling blocks, wheel chocks, and a sewer hose is also wise. For outdoor setup, items such as camping chairs, a foldable table, an awning mat, and outdoor lighting are essential for comfort and convenience.

Safety is paramount, so a well-stocked first-aid kit is non-negotiable. This should include band-aids, antiseptic wipes, bandages, pain relievers, insect repellent, and any personal medications. Additionally, it's important to have a fire extinguisher, a smoke detector, and a carbon monoxide detector in the RV.

Entertainment should not be overlooked. While the primary allure of RV camping is enjoying the outdoors, there will be downtime. Board games, cards, books, and a few digital devices for movies or music can enhance the camping experience. It's also wise to pack outdoor recreational equipment like bikes, hiking gear, or fishing rods, depending on the nature of the trip.

Hygiene is another aspect that requires careful planning. While RVs offer bathroom facilities, packing toiletries, towels, and extra toilet paper is essential. Also, consider the RV's tanks' water usage and capacity when planning showers and other water usage.

Last but not least, it's essential to consider the environmental impact of RV camping. This includes being prepared for waste management with garbage bags, recycling containers, and knowing how to dispose of waste properly at the campsite. Also, bringing reusable dishes and cutlery can help minimize waste.

In conclusion, packing for an RV camping trip is a comprehensive task that requires careful consideration of various aspects. From ensuring the vehicle's readiness to packing for living, sleeping, safety, entertainment, and environmental responsibility, each element plays a vital role in the overall experience. A well-packed RV is the foundation of a successful camping trip, allowing travelers to enjoy the beauty of nature with the comfort and convenience of a home on wheels. With the right preparation and checklist, RV camping can be an enriching experience, offering freedom, adventure, and the opportunity to create lasting memories.

## Tips for efficient space utilization

Traveling in a recreational vehicle (RV) offers a unique blend of adventure and convenience. However, one of the challenges many RV enthusiasts face is the efficient utilization of space. Unlike stationary homes, RVs offer limited square footage, requiring strategic planning and organization to maximize comfort and functionality. This section provides insights into the various methods and strategies to effectively utilize space in an RV, ensuring a more enjoyable and stress-free travel experience.

The essence of efficient space utilization in an RV lies in the 'less is more' principle. The first step is to adopt a minimalist approach. This involves critically assessing what is essential for the trip and what can be left behind. The key is to focus on multipurpose items that can serve more than one function, thus reducing the need for numerous single-use items. For instance, a dining table that converts into a bed or a bench that offers storage space underneath are examples of furniture that serve dual purposes.

Storage is a critical component of space management in an RV. Innovative storage solutions can significantly enhance the living experience in a confined space. Utilizing vertical space is a clever way to increase storage capacity. This can be achieved by installing shelves and hanging organizers. Using the inside of cabinet doors for additional storage, such as installing racks for spices or hooks for utensils, can free up valuable space. Furthermore, under-bed storage, toe-kick drawers, and overhead cabinets are excellent ways to utilize often overlooked spaces.

Another important aspect is the organization of belongings. Assigning a specific place for each item and maintaining this order reduces clutter and makes it easier to find things when needed. This can be particularly important in an RV where space is at a premium. Utilizing storage containers, drawer dividers, and organizers can help maintain this organization. Clear labeling of containers and shelves can also be helpful, especially in shared spaces where multiple people need to find or store items.

The choice of furniture and fittings in an RV can greatly influence the perception of space. Opting for furniture proportionate to the RV's size is essential. Oversized furniture can make the space feel cramped and limit movement. Convertible or collapsible furniture, such as fold-down desks or extendable dining tables, provide flexibility, adapting the space to different needs throughout the day. Similarly, built-in furniture that integrates storage solutions can be a space-efficient choice.

In terms of décor, a few strategic choices can make the RV interior feel more spacious. Light colors for walls, ceilings, and furnishings can create an illusion of more space. Mirrors are also effective in visually expanding the area and enhancing natural light. However, it's essential to strike a balance and avoid over-decorating, as too many decorative items can contribute to a cluttered and confined feeling.

Lighting plays a crucial role in creating a sense of space. Natural light should be maximized wherever possible. Keeping windows unobstructed and using light window treatments can help achieve this. Additionally, using multiple light sources, such as overhead lights, task lights, and accent lights, can help to visually expand the space and create a warm and inviting atmosphere.

The kitchen area in an RV requires special attention regarding space utilization. Using collapsible kitchen items like bowls, colanders, and kettles can save a lot of space. Magnetic strips for knives and metal utensils, and hanging racks for pots and pans, are space-efficient ways to store kitchen essentials. A small, multi-functional appliance like a combination microwave-convection oven can serve multiple purposes while occupying less space.

Choosing bedding that is easy to store during the day, such as sleeping bags or foldable comforters, can free up space in the bedroom area. Using vacuum-seal bags for storing extra bedding and clothing is also a space-saving technique. If the RV design allows, considering a Murphy bed or a loft bed can be a great way to maximize space, providing a sleeping area that can be stowed away when not in use.

Bathroom space in an RV is often limited, so maximizing this area is crucial. Using towel racks that can be attached to doors or walls, and shower caddies for toiletries can help keep the bathroom organized and clutter-free. A small, over-the-toilet cabinet or shelves can provide additional storage space for bathroom essentials. Finally, outdoor living space can effectively extend the living area of an RV. Awnings, foldable chairs, and an outdoor rug can create a comfortable outdoor living area, providing additional space for relaxation and entertainment. This can be particularly beneficial in good weather, allowing the indoors to be used primarily for cooking and sleeping.

In conclusion, efficient space utilization in an RV is a combination of smart planning, organization, and the use of multi-functional items. It involves making the most of every inch of available space through innovative storage solutions, appropriate furniture selection, and strategic interior design. By following these tips, RV travelers can create a comfortable, functional, and enjoyable living space, enhancing their overall travel experience. Effective space management is key to a successful and memorable RV adventure, whether it's a weekend getaway or a long-term journey.

# Maintenance and safety checks before hitting the road

Embarking on a recreational vehicle (RV) journey is an adventure that combines the freedom of the open road with the comforts of home. However, to ensure a safe and enjoyable trip, it is imperative to conduct thorough maintenance and safety checks before setting out. This section discusses the essential steps and considerations for preparing an RV for travel, focusing on maintenance, safety inspections, and practical tips to avoid common issues.

The foundation of a successful RV trip is a well-maintained vehicle. Regular maintenance extends the RV's life and ensures the safety of its occupants and others on the road. The first step in RV maintenance is a comprehensive check of the engine and mechanical systems. This includes inspecting the engine oil, coolant levels, transmission fluid, and brake fluid. It's also essential to examine the condition of the belts, hoses, and engine battery. Ensuring these components are in good working order can prevent breakdowns and costly repairs.

Tires are a critical component of RV safety. Before every trip, inspect the tires for signs of wear, cracks, and proper inflation. Tire pressure should be checked and adjusted according to the manufacturer's specifications, as incorrect tire pressure can lead to poor handling, increased wear, and even blowouts. Don't forget to inspect the spare tire as well, ensuring it is serviceable in case of an emergency.

The braking system is another vital safety feature. Check the brake pads, rotors, and fluid. If the RV has been sitting for an extended period, it's also wise to check for any signs of corrosion or damage. For those towing a vehicle or trailer, ensure the brake connections and lighting systems between the RV and the towed unit are functioning correctly.

RVs, with their complex electrical systems, require careful attention. This includes checking the RV's battery, ensuring it's fully charged and corrosion-free. All lights, both interior and exterior, should be tested. Additionally, inspect the wiring for any signs of damage or wear. For those who rely on generators, ensure they are in good working condition and that you have adequate fuel supplies.

The plumbing system in an RV also needs regular checks. This includes ensuring that all connections are secure and that there are no leaks. The water pump, toilet, and shower should be tested for proper operation. The grey and black water tanks should also be emptied and cleaned regularly to prevent odors and blockages.

RV gas systems used for heating and cooking must be checked for leaks and proper function. This includes inspecting the gas lines, connections, and ensuring that the gas detectors inside the RV are working correctly. It's also essential to check the expiration date on propane tanks and replace them if necessary.

The interior of the RV also demands attention. Ensure that all furniture and appliances are securely fastened to prevent movement while in transit. Windows and doors should be checked to ensure they close and lock properly. Additionally, all items stored inside the RV should be secured to prevent shifting during travel, which can cause damage or injury.

A crucial aspect of RV preparation is ensuring that all safety equipment is in place and functioning. This includes smoke detectors, carbon monoxide detectors, fire extinguishers, and a first-aid kit. These items should be checked regularly and replaced or refilled as necessary.

Beyond the physical checks, reviewing and understanding the RV's weight limits is essential. Overloading an RV can lead to handling problems, increased wear on the vehicle, and can be a severe safety hazard. Ensure the weight distribution is balanced and within the vehicle's specified capacity.

An often-overlooked aspect of RV preparation is documentation. This includes ensuring that the vehicle's registration, insurance, and any necessary permits are current. Additionally, carrying manuals and warranty information can be invaluable during a breakdown or when seeking professional assistance.

Finally, it is advisable for RV owners, especially those new to RVing, to familiarize themselves with the basic troubleshooting and repair techniques. This includes understanding how to change a tire, reset a tripped breaker, and address common issues like a stuck slide-out. Additionally, carrying a well-stocked tool kit and spare parts like fuses and light bulbs can save time and hassle during the trip.

In conclusion, preparing an RV for the road is a comprehensive process that involves meticulous checks and maintenance of various systems and components. From the engine and tires to the plumbing and gas systems, each element plays a crucial role in the safety and functionality of the vehicle. By conducting these checks before each trip, RV owners can ensure that their journey is enjoyable and safe for everyone involved. With proper preparation and a proactive maintenance approach, travelers can confidently explore, knowing that their home on wheels is ready for whatever adventures lie ahead.

# CHAPTER IV

# Navigating the National Parks

## Tips for driving and parking your RV within the parks

Driving and parking a recreational vehicle (RV) within parks can be a challenging yet rewarding experience. The freedom to explore natural landscapes and camp in picturesque settings comes with the responsibility of navigating an oversized vehicle through often unfamiliar and sometimes rugged terrain. This section provides detailed insights and tips for handling and parking an RV within parks, ensuring a safe and enjoyable experience for both the driver and the surrounding environment.

Firstly, it is essential to understand and respect the size and limitations of an RV. These vehicles are significantly larger and heavier than standard automobiles, affecting their handling, turning radius, and braking distance. Before embarking on a journey, drivers should familiarize themselves with the dimensions of their RV, including its height, width, and length. This knowledge is crucial for avoiding low-hanging branches, narrow passages, and other spatial challenges commonly encountered in park settings.

Two of the critical considerations when driving an RV are speed and handling. Given their size, RVs require more time and distance to stop compared to regular vehicles. Therefore, driving at a moderate speed is advisable, allowing ample time to react to road conditions, wildlife, and other hazards. This is particularly important in park areas with winding roads and visibility limited. Drivers should also be mindful of their vehicle's larger blind spots and make use of mirrors and cameras to navigate safely.

Turning and maneuvering an RV requires patience and practice. Wide turns are a necessity due to the vehicle's length. Drivers should approach turns slowly, angling the RV to ensure the tail end does not clip obstacles or veer into oncoming traffic. Additionally, reversing an RV can be challenging, especially into a campsite. Using a spotter outside the vehicle to guide the driver is a helpful strategy to avoid obstacles and position the RV correctly.

Parking an RV in a park requires careful planning and consideration of the surrounding environment. It's essential to choose a campsite that can accommodate the size of the RV. Once a suitable spot is found, the driver must ensure that the RV is parked in a way that does not damage the natural surroundings. This includes avoiding parking on vegetation and staying within designated areas. Leveling the RV is crucial for both comfort and the proper functioning of appliances. Most RVs are equipped with leveling jacks or blocks that can be used to achieve a level position.

When setting up camp, it's essential to consider the location of hookups for electricity, water, and sewage. The RV should be parked close enough to these connections without straining the hoses and cables. Additionally, ensuring that the awnings and slide-outs can be fully extended without encroaching on neighboring campsites or park features is crucial for a harmonious camping experience.

Safety is paramount when parking and setting up an RV. This includes chocking the wheels to prevent the vehicle from rolling and disconnecting the vehicle from the tow vehicle, if applicable, in a secure manner. Before leaving the RV, a thorough check to ensure that all appliances are turned off and the vehicle is locked is a good practice.

In addition to the physical aspects of driving and parking, it's essential to be aware of park regulations. This includes speed limits, driving hours, and specific rules regarding RVs. Many parks have designated areas for RV camping, and adhering to these regulations helps preserve the natural environment and ensures the safety of all park visitors.

Another consideration for RV drivers is the impact of weather conditions. Rain, snow, and ice can significantly affect driving and parking conditions. It's essential to check the weather forecast and be prepared for changing conditions. This might include carrying chains for tires in snowy conditions or seeking shelter during severe weather.

Navigating through tight spaces, such as campground roads and parking spots, can be one of the most challenging aspects of RV camping. Drivers should take their time, use all available aids such as mirrors and cameras, and not hesitate to ask for assistance when needed. Practicing driving and parking in a controlled environment before the trip can also be beneficial, especially for those new to RV camping.

The environmental impact of RV camping should also be considered. This includes being mindful of noise levels, especially when using generators, and ensuring that all waste is disposed of properly. Respecting wildlife and maintaining a safe distance is also crucial for the safety of both the animals and the campers.

In conclusion, driving and parking an RV within parks requires a combination of skill, patience, and respect for the environment. Understanding the vehicle's dimensions and limitations, adhering to park regulations, and being prepared for various challenges are key to a successful RV park experience. With careful planning and consideration, RV camping can be a delightful way to explore and enjoy the natural beauty of parks, creating lasting memories while preserving the environment for future visitors.

## National park entrance fees and passes

Embarking on a journey through national parks in a recreational vehicle (RV) is an experience that offers unparalleled access to the natural wonders of a country. However, navigating the costs associated with such a trip, specifically the entrance fees and passes required for national parks, is an essential aspect of planning. This section explores the various types of fees and passes available for national park visitors traveling by RV, highlighting the importance of understanding these costs for budgeting and trip planning.

The concept of entrance fees and passes for national parks is rooted in the need to maintain and preserve these natural treasures. The revenue generated from these fees is typically used for the upkeep of the parks, including maintaining trails, facilities, and visitor centers, as well as conservation and wildlife protection efforts. Understanding these fees is crucial for RV travelers, as they can vary significantly from one park to another and may differ for vehicles, especially large ones like RVs.

National parks often have a standard entrance fee, which is charged per vehicle. This fee usually covers all passengers within the vehicle and is valid for a specific duration, commonly seven consecutive days. For RV travelers, it's essential to check if there are additional costs based on the size or type of RV, as some parks might charge extra for larger vehicles. Additionally, some parks may have separate fees for additional amenities or activities, such as camping, guided tours, or special events.

One way to manage the cost of visiting multiple parks is by purchasing a national parks pass. In the United States, for instance, the America the Beautiful - National Parks and Federal Recreational Lands Pass offers access to more than 2,000 federal recreation sites, including all national parks. This annual pass is particularly cost-effective for RV travelers planning to visit several parks within a year. The pass covers entrance fees for a driver and all passengers in a personal vehicle at per-vehicle fee areas or up to four adults at sites that charge per person. Children aged 15 or under are admitted free of charge.

There are also special passes available for specific groups of people. For example, senior citizens, military personnel, and persons with disabilities often have access to discounted or free passes. These passes provide the same benefits as the annual pass but are tailored to be more accessible to these groups. It's beneficial for RV travelers who qualify for these passes to acquire them, as they offer substantial savings.

In addition to the federal passes, some states offer their own park passes, which can be an excellent value for those focusing their RV travel within a particular state. These state-specific passes often cover entrance and sometimes additional activity fees within state parks. However, they are not valid for national parks, which are federally managed. It's essential for RV travelers to differentiate between state and national parks when purchasing passes and to plan accordingly.

Another factor to consider is each park's booking and reservation policies, especially for camping. Many national parks offer campgrounds with varying levels of facilities, from basic tent sites to full-service RV hookups. Campsite fees are typically separate from the entrance fee and vary based on the amenities provided. RV travelers should plan and reserve campsites well in advance, especially during peak tourist seasons, as spots can fill up quickly.

It's also wise for RV travelers to be aware of national parks' different seasons and peak times. Entrance fees can vary depending on the time of year, with some parks offering reduced rates or free days during off-peak periods. Taking advantage of these times saves money and provides a more tranquil and less crowded experience.

Understanding the rules and regulations associated with the passes and entrance fees is crucial. For instance, annual passes are generally non-transferable and may require showing a photo ID upon entry. The passes typically cover entrance fees but do not waive other charges such as camping, boat launch, or tour fees. The environmental impact of RV travel in national parks is another consideration. While entrance fees contribute to conservation efforts, RV travelers are responsible for practicing environmentally friendly camping and traveling. This includes adhering to park rules, staying on designated roads and campsites, properly disposing of waste, and being mindful of wildlife and natural resources.

In conclusion, navigating the entrance fees and passes for national parks is vital to planning an RV trip. Understanding the various options available, from annual national passes to specific group discounts, can help travelers budget effectively and enjoy a broader range of parks. Additionally, being mindful of reservation policies, peak seasons, and environmental responsibilities ensures a more enjoyable and sustainable experience. With careful planning and consideration of these factors, RV travelers can fully immerse themselves in the beauty and diversity of national parks, creating memorable adventures on the open road.

# Exploring the park's natural beauty and wildlife

Exploring a park's natural beauty and wildlife is a journey that transcends mere observation; it is an immersive experience that connects us with the primal essence of nature. This section delves into the various facets of exploring parks, focusing on appreciating their natural beauty and their diverse wildlife. It discusses how one can engage with these environments responsibly and gain a deeper understanding and appreciation of the natural world.

The allure of a park's natural beauty lies in its unspoiled landscapes, ranging from towering mountains and dense forests to serene lakes and rolling meadows. Each of these environments presents a unique ecosystem, teeming with life and natural phenomena. To truly appreciate a park's beauty, engaging with it mindfully and respectfully is essential. This involves adhering to established trails and guidelines designed not only for visitor safety but also to protect the environment from the impact of human activity.

One of the most rewarding aspects of exploring a park is observing wildlife in its natural habitat. Each creature plays a vital role in the ecosystem, from the smallest insects to the largest mammals. Observing these animals requires patience, silence, and a keen eye. Early mornings or late evenings are often the best times for wildlife spotting, as many animals are most active during these cooler parts of the day.

Birdwatching is a particularly popular activity in many parks. Armed with a pair of binoculars and a field guide, visitors can enjoy identifying various bird species while appreciating their behaviors and songs. Similarly, parks with aquatic environments offer the chance to see different wildlife, including fish, amphibians, and water birds. Each park has its own set of species, making every wildlife watching experience unique.

Photography is a wonderful way to capture the beauty of the park and its inhabitants. It allows one to preserve and share memories of the experience with others. However, it's essential to prioritize the welfare of the wildlife and environment over getting the perfect shot. This means maintaining a safe distance from animals and not disturbing their natural behaviors or habitats.

To deepen the exploration experience, many parks offer guided tours and educational programs. These can provide valuable insights into the history of the park, the intricacies of its ecosystems, and the behaviors of its wildlife. Park rangers and naturalists can offer a wealth of knowledge, often sharing fascinating facts and stories that enrich the visit.

For a more immersive experience, camping within the park can be a remarkable way to connect with nature. Spending a night under the stars, surrounded by the sounds of the wilderness, can be a profound and unforgettable experience. However, it's crucial to practice responsible camping by following Leave No Trace principles, ensuring that one's presence does not harm the environment.

Hiking is another way to explore the park's natural beauty. It allows one to traverse different landscapes, encounter various wildlife habitats, and witness stunning vistas. Hiking ranges from short, easy trails to challenging backcountry treks, catering to various abilities and interests. Regardless of the trail's difficulty, it's essential to be prepared with appropriate gear, water, and a map or GPS device.

For those interested in the aquatic aspects of a park, activities like kayaking, canoeing, or snorkeling can offer a unique perspective on the park's ecosystems. These activities allow visitors to glide along rivers, lakes, or coastal waters, observing life both above and below the waterline. As with all activities in natural settings, it's important to respect wildlife and practice safety, including wearing life jackets and being aware of weather conditions.

The changing seasons can dramatically alter the landscape and wildlife behaviors in parks, offering different experiences throughout the year. For instance, spring might bring wildflower blooms and newborn wildlife, while autumn could offer spectacular foliage displays. Visiting a park during different seasons can provide a deeper appreciation of the natural cycles and transformations that occur.

In addition to exploring the natural beauty, understanding and respecting the park's cultural heritage is also essential. Many parks are situated in areas of significant historical or cultural importance, and some may be sacred sites for indigenous communities. Learning about the cultural significance of these areas can add a layer of depth to the exploration experience.

Finally, exploring a park's natural beauty and wildlife is about what one sees, learns, and feels. It's an opportunity to disconnect from the distractions of modern life and reconnect with nature. It can be a time for reflection, relaxation, and rejuvenation. The natural world's sights, sounds, and smells can have a profoundly calming and restorative effect, reminding us of our place within the greater tapestry of life.

In conclusion, exploring a park's natural beauty and wildlife is an enriching experience that offers both physical and spiritual rewards. It requires a respectful and mindful approach to preserve these natural wonders for future generations. Whether through wildlife watching, photography, hiking, or simply sitting and observing, each encounter with nature in a park can deepen our appreciation for the world around us and our role in protecting it. As we venture into these beautiful and wild places, we are reminded of the intricate and delicate balance of life and the importance of our stewardship of the planet.

# CHAPTER V

# Setting Up Camp

## How to properly set up your RV at the campsite

The process of setting up a recreational vehicle (RV) at a campsite requires a combination of organizing, having technical expertise, and adding a touch of personal flair. Not only is this technique essential for assuring the safety and functionality of your recreational vehicle (RV), but it is also essential for ensuring that your camping trip is comfortable and enjoyable. The purpose of this section is to provide a complete overview of how to correctly set up a recreational vehicle (RV) at a campsite, highlighting the most important processes and factors involved in this process.

As soon as you get at the campsite, the first thing you should do is select the ideal location for putting up your recreational vehicle. This decision ought to be based on a number of criteria, such as the levelness of the ground, the closeness to hookups (if they are accessible), and the quantity of sunlight or shade that is wanted. It is also essential to take into account the dimensions and orientation of the site in relation to your recreational vehicle (RV), making certain that there is sufficient room for all slide-outs and awnings, as well as for activities that take place outside.

After a location that is suitable has been chosen, the following step is to level the recreational vehicle. This is a very important step because an uneven RV can cause a variety of issues, including doors that swing shut abruptly, difficulty sleeping, and even problems with your refrigerator. In the absence of built-in leveling systems, manual leveling blocks or jacks can be utilized. The majority of contemporary recreational vehicles (RVs) come equipped with such systems. Not only does ensuring that your recreational vehicle (RV) is level increase comfort, but it also reduces unnecessary strain on the construction and components of the vehicle.

Following the leveling of the recreational vehicle, the following step is to chock the wheels. Especially when the recreational vehicle is not connected to a tow vehicle, this is a precautionary action that is taken to prevent the RV from rolling. It is important to position wheel chocks so that they are pressed against both sides of the tires. Another essential stage in the process of setting up is connecting to the respective utilities. If your campsite offers hookups, you'll want to connect to these amenities. Make the initial connection between the RV and the electrical hookup by utilizing the power cable of your RV and any adapters that may be required. It is essential to look into whether or not the power supply at the campground is compatible with the electrical system of your recreational vehicle. The next step in the water hookup process is to connect a hose from the water supply at the campsite to your recreational vehicle. When it comes to protecting the plumbing system of your recreational vehicle (RV), it is strongly suggested that you make use of a water pressure regulator and a certified drinking water hose. Last but not least, if there is a sewage hookup available, you should connect the sewer hose of your RV to the drain of the campsite using the necessary fittings. This will ensure that the connection is both tight and secure, which will avoid leaks.

It is time to begin preparing the interior of the RV once it has been connected to the utilities. In order to accomplish this, you will need to unpack and organize your possessions, establish sleeping places, and make sure that everything is within its proper location. This is also a good opportunity to turn on any appliances that you will use during your stay, such as the refrigerator, the heating or air conditioning system, and any other heating or cooling systems.

Setting up the exterior of your recreational vehicle is also very important. The creation of a suitable outside living room can be accomplished by extension of awnings, placement of chairs, and installation of an outdoor rug. Additionally, this is the time to put up any outside cooking equipment or leisure things such as kayaks or bicycles from the previous step.

When it comes to the process of setting up, safety inspections should not be neglected. Checking that all of the appliances are operating properly and safely, verifying that the smoke and carbon monoxide detectors are functioning properly, and becoming familiar with the location of fire extinguishers and emergency exits are all part of this process.

Managing garbage in an appropriate manner is an essential component of RV camping. Not only does this involve correctly connecting to sewer hookups, but it also involves handling garbage and recycling responsibilities. When it comes to garbage disposal, campgrounds often have specific locations allocated for that purpose. It is essential to adhere to the standards provided by the campground in order to keep the environment clean and risk-free.

After everything has been set up, it is absolutely necessary to observe the laws and etiquette of the campground. The observance of quiet hours, the maintenance of a clean campsite, and the consideration of one's neighbors are all included in this measure. It is important to adhere to these principles in order to make sure that everyone at the campground has a great time.

Last but not least, it is essential to make time to sit back and appreciate your surroundings. Whether you want to unwind outside of your recreational vehicle (RV), explore the park, or take part in activities offered by the campground, the true essence of RV camping resides in the experiences and memories you create during your time there.

In conclusion, the process of correctly setting up your recreational vehicle (RV) at a campsite is a multi-step procedure that involves a combination of certain technical steps and personal touches. There are a number of steps that contribute significantly to the entire camping experience. These include choosing the appropriate location, ensuring that the RV is level, connecting the utilities, and establishing a comfortable living space. By according to these instructions, you will be able to ensure that your recreational vehicle (RV) is set up in a secure and comfortable manner, which will enable you to fully enjoy the benefits of RV camping. Spending the effort to correctly set up your recreational vehicle (RV) can result in a camping trip that is more pleasurable, safer, and more memorable for you, regardless of whether you are an experienced RV enthusiast or a first-time camper.

## Campfire safety and Leave No Trace principles

A campfire can be the heart of an RV camping trip, providing warmth, light, and a communal space for sharing stories and cooking food. However, it also carries a significant responsibility for safety and environmental stewardship. Coupled with the Leave No Trace principles, maintaining campfire safety is essential for preserving the natural environment and ensuring the well-being of all campers and wildlife. This section explores the importance of campfire safety and the integration of Leave No Trace principles during an RV trip.

Campfire safety begins with understanding and adhering to the regulations of the camping area. Different parks and campgrounds have specific rules about when and where fires are permitted, often depending on the season, weather conditions, and fire danger levels. Before lighting a fire, it's imperative to check with local park officials or campground hosts to ensure compliance with current regulations. In areas where campfires are allowed, using designated fire rings or pits is crucial for containing the fire and minimizing its impact on the surrounding area.

The selection of firewood is a key component of campfire safety. Bringing locally sourced firewood or purchasing it from the campground is recommended to prevent the spread of invasive insects and diseases that can devastate forests. Using only dead and downed wood found near the campsite is also acceptable in some areas, but it's important to never cut branches from live trees, as this damages the ecosystem and is often illegal.

Once the fire is permitted, and the appropriate wood is sourced, the next step is building and lighting the fire safely. It's essential to keep the fire small and manageable, which minimizes the risk of it becoming uncontrollable and reduces the amount of smoke and ash produced. When lighting the fire, use matches or a lighter and avoid flammable liquids, which can create dangerous flare-ups. Keeping water, a shovel, or a fire extinguisher nearby is a good practice in case the fire needs to be extinguished quickly.

As the fire burns, it's essential to never leave it unattended. A breeze can quickly carry sparks to nearby vegetation, potentially starting a wildfire. Children and pets should be supervised around the fire, ensuring they stay at a safe distance. Additionally, it's essential to avoid burning trash or food items in the fire, as this can attract wildlife and release harmful toxins into the air.

It should be done thoroughly and responsibly when it's time to extinguish the fire. Dousing the fire with water, stirring the ashes, and applying more water is the most effective method. The fire should be completely out and cool to the touch before leaving the site. This practice ensures that no residual embers can reignite or spread.

Leave No Trace principles are closely aligned with campfire safety and extend to all aspects of RV camping. These principles are designed to minimize the environmental impact of camping activities and preserve the natural beauty and integrity of the outdoors. The first principle, Plan Ahead and Prepare, involves understanding the regulations and unique concerns of the area you plan to visit, including fire regulations. It's essential to prepare for extreme weather, hazards, and emergencies.

Traveling and Camping on Durable Surfaces is another key principle. This means sticking to established trails and campsites, avoiding creating new trails or expanding campsites. When setting up camp, it's essential to keep the RV and all gear on surfaces that are resistant to damage, such as gravel or established grassy areas. Disposing of Waste Properly is crucial in preserving the natural environment. This includes packing out all trash and leftover food, cleaning up after pets, and using bathroom facilities or following proper procedures for human waste disposal. It's also important to wash dishes and bathe at least 200 feet away from streams or lakes to protect water sources.

Leaving What You Find is a principle that encourages campers to preserve their surroundings' natural and cultural features. This means not removing rocks, plants, and other natural objects, and avoiding introducing or transporting non-native species.

Minimizing Campfire Impacts, as discussed, is vital for both safety and environmental protection. This principle extends to using a stove for cooking when possible and keeping fires small when they are permitted.

Respecting Wildlife is another crucial aspect of Leave No Trace. This means observing wildlife from a distance, not feeding animals, and storing food securely to avoid attracting wildlife to the campsite.

Lastly, Being Considerate of Other Visitors ensures that everyone can enjoy their outdoor experience. This includes keeping noise levels down, respecting other campers' privacy, and controlling pets.

In conclusion, adhering to campfire safety guidelines and the Leave No Trace principles is essential during an RV trip. These practices ensure campers' safety and the natural environment's protection. By following these guidelines, RV campers can enjoy the unique experience of a campfire while maintaining the pristine beauty of the outdoors for future generations to enjoy. It's a balance of enjoying the present while safeguarding the future, a responsibility every camper should embrace.

## Establishing a comfortable and functional campsite

Embarking on an RV trip offers a delightful blend of adventure and comfort, allowing travelers to explore the great outdoors while enjoying the conveniences of home. The key to maximizing this experience lies in establishing a comfortable and functional campsite. This section explores the various aspects of setting up an ideal RV campsite, from selecting the right location to organizing living spaces and ensuring environmental responsibility.

Choosing the right campsite is the first crucial step in this process. The ideal location depends on individual preferences and the type of RV. Factors to consider include the size of the site, its proximity to amenities, the level of privacy, and accessibility to points of interest.

Some campers prefer sites close to bathrooms and showers for convenience, while others might prioritize a more secluded spot further from communal areas for peace and tranquility. Additionally, the site's orientation can impact exposure to sun and wind, which can be significant depending on the season and climate.

Once the site is chosen, the next step is to position and level the RV. Ensuring that the RV is level is critical for both comfort and the proper functioning of certain appliances, like refrigerators. Leveling blocks or built-in leveling systems can be used to achieve this. Proper positioning also involves considering the placement of slide-outs and awnings, ensuring they can be fully extended without encroaching on neighboring sites or natural vegetation.

Setting up a functional outdoor living area is essential to RV camping. This can include unfolding chairs, setting up a table, and laying out an outdoor mat to define the space. An awning or canopy provides shade and protection from the elements, creating a comfortable area to relax, dine, or socialize. Outdoor lighting, such as string lights or solar-powered lamps, can enhance the ambiance and safety of the site after dark.

The next consideration is the organization of the interior space of the RV. Efficient use of space is key, utilizing built-in storage solutions and adding organizers where necessary to keep belongings tidy and accessible. This includes designating specific areas for sleeping, dining, and lounging, and ensuring that pathways are clear to move easily throughout the RV. The goal is to create a living space that is cozy yet uncluttered.

A well-organized kitchen area is crucial for a functional campsite. This includes stocking the kitchen with necessary cookware, utensils, and food supplies. Planning meals in advance can help in organizing these supplies efficiently. Where permitted, outdoor cooking options like grills or campfires can also add to the camping experience while reducing heat and odors inside the RV.

Sanitation and hygiene are important considerations, especially in self-contained RVs without direct access to campsite facilities. This involves efficiently managing water usage for cooking, cleaning, and bathing, especially when staying at sites without hookups. Proper waste disposal is also crucial, including regular emptying of holding tanks at designated dump stations and ensuring trash is disposed of responsibly.

Safety at the campsite is paramount. This includes securing the RV, locking doors and windows when away, and safely storing valuables. A well-stocked first-aid kit should be readily accessible, along with fire extinguishers and other emergency supplies. Additionally, familiarizing oneself with the campsite's emergency procedures and weather conditions is advisable.

Connectivity and entertainment, though often secondary, are essential for many RV campers. This might involve setting up satellite dishes, antennas, or Wi-Fi boosters, depending on the level of connectivity desired. Bringing along books, games, and outdoor recreational equipment can enhance the camping experience, especially during extended stays.

Environmental responsibility is an integral part of establishing a campsite. Adhering to the Leave No Trace principles, such as minimizing the impact on the land, respecting wildlife, and leaving the site as found or better, is essential. This includes avoiding the disturbance of natural features and wildlife, using eco-friendly products, and practicing efficient energy use.

Lastly, creating a personalized touch can make the campsite feel like a home away from home. This can include adding decorative elements like outdoor rugs, lanterns, or potted plants. Personalizing the space to reflect individual styles and preferences can enhance the overall enjoyment of the camping experience.

In conclusion, establishing a comfortable and functional campsite during an RV trip involves careful planning and thoughtful organization. It starts with selecting the appropriate campsite and extends to setting up a living space that balances comfort, functionality, and environmental responsibility. By paying attention to these details, RV campers can create a welcoming and enjoyable environment that enhances their travel experience, allowing them to fully immerse themselves in the joys of the outdoors while maintaining the conveniences of modern living. With a well-set-up campsite, the RV trip becomes not just a journey but a memorable and comfortable outdoor adventure.

# CHAPTER VI

# Cooking and Dining

## RV kitchen essentials

The kitchen in a recreational vehicle (RV) is a marvel of efficiency and compactness, serving as the heart of the mobile home. Cooking and dining in an RV, while a unique experience, requires a well-thought-out kitchen equipped with essentials that maximize space without sacrificing functionality. This section delves into the essential components of an RV kitchen, discussing how to maintain convenience and comfort in a limited space.

Firstly, the importance of space-saving appliances cannot be overstated in an RV kitchen. Given the limited space, each appliance must be chosen for its compactness and multi-functionality. A good example is a combination microwave-convection oven, which allows for various cooking methods without occupying too much space. Similarly, a compact two-burner stove is often sufficient for most RV cooking needs, and when paired with a small, efficient refrigerator, forms the core of the RV kitchen. Some RVs also come equipped with a small dishwasher, which is a luxury that can save time and water, a precious resource when on the road.

Cookware and utensils in an RV kitchen need to be carefully selected. Space-saving features are invaluable, such as nesting bowls and pots, collapsible colanders, and foldable dish racks. Opting for multi-purpose utensils can also minimize clutter. For instance, a spatula with a built-in bottle opener or stackable measuring cups can be incredibly useful. Quality should not be sacrificed for size;

however, durable and easy-to-clean materials like stainless steel and silicone are ideal for the RV lifestyle.

Storage solutions are critical in an RV kitchen. Innovative ideas such as magnetic spice racks, under-shelf baskets, and over-the-cabinet door organizers can greatly maximize limited space. Utilizing vertical space with hanging racks for pots and utensils can keep the countertops clear. Clear, stackable storage containers help organize pantry items, save space, and keep food fresh.

The design of the kitchen must also take into consideration the need for efficiency and ease of movement. This means a well-planned layout where the stove, sink, and refrigerator are placed for optimal workflow. The arrangement should allow easy access to appliances and storage while cooking, with enough countertop space for meal preparation. In many RVs, kitchen counters are designed to be multipurpose, doubling as dining areas or workspaces.

Dishware and glassware in an RV kitchen should be chosen for their durability and ability to withstand the rigors of travel. Melamine dishes are popular as they are lightweight, unbreakable, and come in various designs. Similarly, acrylic or silicone wine glasses and cups can prevent breakage. However, for those who prefer traditional glass or ceramic, careful storage in padded compartments is essential to avoid damage during transit.

Water management is a key consideration in an RV kitchen. Conserving water is often necessary, especially when camping without hookups. This means being mindful of water usage when washing dishes and cooking. Installing a water filter can also be a good investment, ensuring access to clean drinking water without the need for plastic bottles.

A coffee maker is often considered an essential appliance in an RV kitchen for many travelers. However, space and power considerations should guide the choice. Compact, manual coffee makers, like a French press or a stovetop espresso maker, can be more practical than electric coffee machines, especially when boondocking without electrical hookups.

Another aspect to consider is the RV kitchen's ventilation. Cooking can produce a lot of moisture and odors, which, in the confined space of an RV, can become a problem. Ensuring good ventilation with a range hood or an exhaust fan is essential to keep the air fresh and reduce condensation.

Safety in the RV kitchen is paramount. This includes ensuring that all appliances are securely installed and that gas stoves have proper ventilation to prevent carbon monoxide buildup. It's also essential to have a fire extinguisher easily accessible in the kitchen area.

Finally, personalizing the RV kitchen can make the cooking experience more enjoyable. Adding small touches like decorative kitchen towels, a favorite coffee mug, or a piece of art can make the space feel homely. These personal touches can transform the RV kitchen from a functional space into a cozy corner of your mobile home.

In conclusion, outfitting an RV kitchen requires balancing space efficiency, functionality, and personal style. Selecting multi-functional and space-saving appliances and utensils, implementing creative storage solutions, and being mindful of water usage and safety can transform a small kitchen space into an efficient and enjoyable cooking area. With the right setup, an RV kitchen can be just as comfortable and functional as a traditional kitchen, making the RV experience both delightful and convenient. Whether preparing a simple breakfast or a gourmet meal, a well-equipped RV kitchen is central to the joy of RV living and traveling.

# Campfire cooking and recipes

Campfire cooking is an art that turns a simple meal into an engaging, flavorful experience, especially during an RV trip. It's about more than just food; it's about the atmosphere, the warmth of the fire, and the joy of sharing a meal in the great outdoors. This section explores the essentials of campfire cooking, offering practical tips and delightful recipes suited for an RV adventure.

The foundation of campfire cooking lies in mastering the fire itself. Building a campfire suitable for cooking requires more than just igniting logs. It involves creating a steady, controllable heat source. Start by gathering dry wood and kindling, arranging them in a teepee or log cabin structure for good air circulation. Once the fire is lit and burning strongly, wait until it settles down to a bed of glowing coals. This is the ideal heat for cooking, providing a consistent and controllable temperature.

Safety is paramount in campfire cooking. Always check if campfires are permitted in the area and understand the fire regulations of the campsite. Keep a bucket of water or a fire extinguisher nearby in case of emergencies, and ensure the fire is completely extinguished before leaving the site or going to bed.

The choice of cooking equipment is crucial in campfire cooking. Cast iron cookware is highly recommended due to its durability and even heat distribution. A cast iron skillet or Dutch oven can be used for various recipes, from frying to baking. For those who prefer grilling, a sturdy grill grate placed over the fire is essential. Other valuable tools include long-handled tongs, a spatula, and heat-resistant gloves for safe handling of hot cookware.

The versatility of campfire cooking is one of its greatest appeals. It allows for various cooking methods, including grilling, frying, boiling, and even baking. Simple recipes often work best, emphasizing fresh ingredients and straightforward preparation. One classic campfire recipe is the foil packet, also known as a hobo pack. Ingredients like diced meat, vegetables, and seasonings are wrapped in a foil packet and placed in the embers of the fire to cook. This method seals in flavor and moisture, resulting in a delicious, fuss-free meal.

Another campfire favorite is skewers or kebabs. Pieces of meat, vegetables, and even fruits can be threaded onto skewers and grilled over the open flame. This not only cooks the food but also imparts a delightful smoky flavor. Marinades and seasonings can be used to enhance the taste. A simple yet tasty option is a combination of chicken, bell peppers, onions, and mushrooms, marinated in a mixture of olive oil, garlic, lemon juice, and herbs.

For breakfast, a cast iron skillet can be used to cook classics like bacon, eggs, and pancakes. The even heat of the skillet ensures perfectly cooked, flavorful food. Pancakes cooked over a campfire, perhaps with added blueberries or chocolate chips, can be a delightful morning treat.

Campfire cooking also lends itself well to hearty stews and soups. A Dutch oven can be placed directly in the coals, simmering ingredients slowly over several hours. A simple beef stew with potatoes, carrots, onions, and a rich broth can be both comforting and satisfying after a day of outdoor activities.

Desserts are not to be forgotten in campfire cooking. The traditional s'mores, made with roasted marshmallows, chocolate, and graham crackers, are a perennial favorite. For something different, try baking apples wrapped in foil with cinnamon, sugar, and a dollop of butter, creating a delicious, caramelized treat.

In addition to these recipes, creativity and experimentation can lead to various delightful meals. Consider the local produce and regional specialties that can inspire your campfire cooking. Freshly caught fish, local vegetables, and fruits can all be incorporated into your menu.

While cooking, it's essential to keep an eye on food safety. This includes storing perishable items in a cooler with ice, keeping raw and cooked foods separate, and ensuring meats are cooked to the right temperature. A food thermometer can be a handy tool in this regard.

Cleanup after campfire cooking is as important as the preparation. All cookware and utensils should be cleaned thoroughly to avoid attracting wildlife. Dispose of trash and leftovers properly, adhering to the campsite's guidelines. Leaving no trace should be a key principle in all camping activities.

In conclusion, campfire cooking is an enriching aspect of RV trips, blending culinary art with the beauty of the outdoors. It's an opportunity to slow down, savor simple pleasures, and connect with nature and fellow travelers. Whether it's a foil packet dinner, a skillet breakfast, or a Dutch oven stew, campfire recipes can be as diverse and adventurous as your journey. With the right preparation, equipment, and respect for safety and the environment, campfire cooking can elevate your RV experience, creating memories that are as warm and inviting as the fire itself.

## Food storage and handling tips

Managing food storage and handling during an RV trip is a crucial aspect that can significantly impact the overall experience. Effective food management ensures not only the safety and health of the travelers but also contributes to the enjoyment of the journey. This section delves into the key strategies for proper food storage and handling in an RV's limited and dynamic environment.

First and foremost, understanding the limitations and capabilities of your RV's storage facilities is vital. Most RVs have a refrigerator and freezer, which are smaller than standard household versions. Before embarking on the trip, it's essential to test the refrigerator to ensure it's functioning efficiently. The fridge should be pre-cooled a day before the trip, and perishable items should be chilled beforehand to maintain their freshness.

In organizing the refrigerator, a system of categorization is useful. Grouping items together, such as dairy, meats, vegetables, and condiments, aids in easy access and minimizes the time the fridge door stays open. Using clear, airtight containers not only keeps food fresh but also helps to prevent spills and odors. Moreover, it's important to avoid overpacking the refrigerator, as this impedes cold air circulation and can lead to uneven cooling.

Dry storage in an RV requires thoughtful planning. Utilizing cabinetry and pantry spaces efficiently is key. Non-perishable items such as canned goods, pasta, rice, and snacks are staples for RV trips and should be stored to maximize space and accessibility. Stackable storage containers and organizers can be extremely helpful in keeping these items orderly and easily accessible. It's also essential to consider the weight and distribution of stored items, as heavy items should be placed in lower cabinets to maintain the balance and safety of the RV. Another important consideration is the handling and preparation of food. Cross-contamination is a risk, particularly in the small confines of an RV kitchen. Keeping raw and cooked foods separate, using different cutting boards for meats and vegetables, and thoroughly washing hands and utensils are fundamental practices to prevent foodborne illnesses.

Temperature management is crucial in food safety. A reliable thermometer is a necessary tool for an RV kitchen. It's vital to ensure that the refrigerator is running at a safe temperature, typically below 40°F (4°C) for the fridge and 0°F (-18°C) for the freezer. When cooking, it's equally important to ensure that foods, especially meats, are cooked to the appropriate internal temperatures to eliminate harmful bacteria.

For longer trips where replenishing fresh produce isn't feasible, consider alternatives like frozen vegetables and fruits, which can be just as nutritious as their fresh counterparts. Dehydrated or freeze-dried foods are also excellent options as they are lightweight, space-saving, and have a long shelf life.

In dealing with leftovers, prompt refrigeration is vital. Leftovers should be stored in airtight containers and consumed within a few days to prevent spoilage. Labeling leftovers with the date they were cooked is also a good practice to keep track of their freshness.

For outdoor cooking and dining, proper food handling remains essential. Foods meant to be cooked outside should be transported in coolers with sufficient ice or ice packs to maintain a cold temperature. When grilling or cooking over a campfire, it's essential to ensure that the foods reach safe temperatures and are consumed immediately after cooking.

Water management is another critical aspect of food handling in an RV. Using clean, potable water for cooking and cleaning is essential. If the purity of the water source is in question, it should be boiled before use or treated with water purification tablets. It's also prudent to conserve water, especially when dry camping without a direct water hookup.

Effective waste management complements proper food storage and handling. All food scraps and garbage should be disposed of properly to avoid attracting wildlife. Many RV campsites offer designated disposal areas for waste and recycling, and it's essential to utilize these facilities responsibly.

Lastly, being prepared for emergencies is part of responsible food management. This includes having a well-stocked pantry with non-perishable items that can sustain you in case of unexpected events or travel delays. Also, maintaining emergency food and water supply is advisable, especially for remote or off-grid camping.

In conclusion, managing food storage and handling on an RV trip requires careful planning, organization, and adherence to food safety practices. By understanding and efficiently utilizing the available storage space, maintaining proper temperature control, practicing safe food handling, and being prepared for emergencies, RV travelers can ensure that their culinary experiences are enjoyable and safe. Whether it's a weekend getaway or an extended journey, effective food management is critical to a successful and memorable RV adventure.

# CHAPTER VII

# Outdoor Activities

## Hiking and backpacking in national parks

Exploring national parks through hiking and backpacking is a quintessential activity that complements the RV experience. It allows travelers to immerse themselves in these protected areas' natural beauty and rugged wilderness. This section delves into the planning, preparation, and execution of hiking and backpacking in national parks during an RV trip, emphasizing safety, enjoyment, and respect for the environment.

The allure of hiking in national parks lies in their diverse landscapes - from towering mountain peaks and dense forests to vast deserts and serene lakes. Each park offers a unique array of trails, catering to a wide range of abilities and interests. For RV travelers, incorporating hiking into their itinerary requires careful planning. Researching the national park in advance is essential. This includes understanding the geography, weather conditions, and trail options. National park websites, guidebooks, and visitor centers are invaluable resources for gathering this information.

Selecting the right trails is a critical decision that should be based on the physical fitness and experience levels of the hikers, as well as time constraints and personal interests. National parks typically offer a range of trails, from short, easy nature walks to challenging multi-day backpacking trips. It's important to assess your capabilities and prepare accordingly realistically. For those new to hiking or with limited time, shorter day hikes are a great way to experience the park's highlights.

Preparation for hiking in national parks goes beyond physical readiness. The right gear is essential for a safe and comfortable experience. This includes sturdy hiking boots, weather-appropriate clothing, a reliable backpack, and basic navigational tools like a map, compass, or GPS device. Additional gear, such as a tent, sleeping bag, and appropriate food and water supplies, are necessary for longer hikes or backpacking trips.

Safety is paramount in any outdoor adventure, and hiking in national parks is no exception. Before setting out, inform someone of your hiking plan, including the trails you intend to hike and your expected return time. Checking in with park rangers can provide valuable insights into current trail conditions and any potential hazards. It's also important to be aware of wildlife in the area and understand how to coexist safely with the animals you may encounter.

Water management is crucial to hiking, especially in more remote or arid parks. Carrying enough water and understanding methods to purify natural water sources are essential skills. Dehydration can be a serious risk, particularly in hot weather or at high altitudes.

Navigation skills are equally important. While many trails in national parks are well-marked, reading a map and using a compass or GPS device is invaluable, especially in more remote or less-traveled areas. Understanding your route and being aware of landmarks are key to avoiding getting lost.

For those embarking on backpacking trips, additional considerations come into play. Backpacking allows for a deeper exploration of the parks, often leading to less crowded and more pristine areas. However, it requires a higher level of preparation and self-sufficiency. Packing lightweight, calorie-dense food, a suitable tent, a comfortable sleeping bag, and a portable stove are just a few of the necessities. Obtaining the necessary permits, often required for overnight stays in backcountry areas, is also a crucial step.

Leave No Trace principles are fundamental in hiking and backpacking. This set of guidelines promotes responsible outdoor activities that minimize environmental impact. They include principles such as planning ahead and preparing, traveling and camping on durable surfaces, disposing of waste properly, and respecting wildlife. Adhering to these principles ensures that the natural beauty and integrity of the parks are preserved for future generations.

After a day of hiking, returning to the comfort of an RV can be deeply satisfying. The mobility of an RV allows hikers to explore different areas of a park or multiple parks during a single trip. The ability to carry more supplies and gear in an RV also makes it easier to tackle a variety of hiking experiences.

In conclusion, hiking and backpacking in national parks during an RV trip is an enriching experience that allows travelers to connect with nature on a deeper level. It requires careful planning, preparation, and respect for the environment. By choosing the right trails, preparing appropriately, prioritizing safety, and adhering to Leave No Trace principles, RV travelers can immerse themselves in national parks' breathtaking landscapes and diverse ecosystems. Whether it's a leisurely day hike or an adventurous backpacking journey, the combination of RV travel and hiking offers an unparalleled opportunity to explore and appreciate the natural wonders of the great outdoors.

# Biking, fishing, and other recreational activities

Recreational vehicles (RVs) offer the unique opportunity to bring the comforts of home to the great outdoors. Beyond the joy of travel and exploration, RV trips can be enhanced by various recreational activities like biking, fishing, and more. These activities not only enrich the travel experience but also provide opportunities for exercise, relaxation, and closer engagement with nature. This section explores the integration of biking, fishing, and other activities into an RV trip, discussing how they can be planned and enjoyed to their fullest.

Biking is popular among RV enthusiasts, offering a perfect blend of physical exercise and exploration. Many national parks and campgrounds feature extensive biking trails ranging from easy, scenic routes to challenging mountain biking paths. Bringing bikes on an RV trip allows travelers to cover more ground than on foot, enjoying the beauty of the surroundings more intimately than from the vehicle. Modern RVs often come equipped with bike racks, making it easier to transport bicycles. Alternatively, foldable bikes are a space-saving option that can be stored inside the RV.

When planning to include biking in an RV trip, it's essential to research the biking trails in the areas you plan to visit. Understanding the difficulty level, terrain, and length of the trails ensures you are adequately prepared. Safety is paramount, so helmets, knee pads, and other protective gear should be included. It's also wise to carry a basic repair kit for minor bike maintenance issues that might arise.

Fishing is another activity that pairs wonderfully with RV trips, offering a peaceful and rewarding way to connect with nature. Many campgrounds are located near rivers, lakes, or coastal areas that provide excellent fishing opportunities. Fishing can be as simple as casting a line from the shore or as involved as setting off in a boat for deeper waters. It's a versatile activity that can be enjoyed alone for solitude or with family and friends for a fun, shared experience.

Before heading out on a fishing expedition during an RV trip, it's essential to familiarize yourself with the local fishing regulations. This includes obtaining the necessary fishing licenses and understanding catch limits and size restrictions. Bringing along the appropriate fishing gear, such as rods, reels, bait, and tackle, is essential. Additionally, consider how you will store your catch, especially if you plan to keep it – a cooler or a refrigerator in the RV can be handy for this purpose.

Apart from biking and fishing, numerous other activities can be enjoyed during an RV trip. Hiking is a natural choice, allowing travelers to explore diverse landscapes and ecosystems up close. Many RV campers also enjoy bird watching, which can be a serene and educational experience, especially in areas rich in wildlife.

Water sports like kayaking, canoeing, and paddleboarding are excellent additions to an RV trip, mainly when staying near water bodies. These activities provide a fun workout and offer a unique perspective of the landscape from the water. For those who love adrenaline-fueled adventures, activities like rock climbing or zip-lining can be sought out in specific destinations.

When planning these activities, it's crucial to consider your RV's space and weight limitations. Equipment for water sports or climbing can take up significant space, so it's essential to plan accordingly. Renting equipment at your destination is a convenient option that can alleviate the need to carry bulky items.

Another aspect of incorporating recreational activities into an RV trip is the opportunity to learn new skills or hobbies. Photography, for instance, is a hobby that many RV travelers find rewarding. The diverse landscapes and experiences encountered on an RV trip provide ample material for stunning photography, from sweeping landscapes to intimate wildlife shots.

Stargazing is another activity that can be profoundly rewarding, especially in remote areas away from city lights. Many national parks offer dark sky preserves where one can observe the night sky in its full glory. Bringing along a telescope or even just a blanket to lie on can make for an unforgettable night under the stars.

For families traveling in an RV, recreational activities can be an excellent way to bond and create lasting memories. Simple pleasures like flying a kite, playing frisbee, or even setting up a scavenger hunt can provide hours of entertainment. Educational activities like visiting historical sites or nature centers can also enrich children and adults' experiences.

Finally, it's vital to approach all activities with a mindset of respect for the environment. Practicing Leave No Trace principles, being mindful of wildlife, and adhering to park rules and regulations help preserve these natural spaces for future generations to enjoy.

In conclusion, incorporating biking, fishing, and other recreational activities into an RV trip can significantly enhance the experience. These activities provide a deeper connection with nature, physical activity and relaxation opportunities, and the joy of learning new skills. By planning carefully, respecting the environment, and embracing the spirit of adventure, RV travelers can create a journey that is as diverse and fulfilling as the landscapes they traverse. Whether it's riding along a mountain trail, casting a line into a tranquil lake, or simply enjoying a night under the stars, these experiences add depth and richness to the RV adventure.

# Tips for staying safe in the wilderness

Embarking on an RV trip into the wilderness offers a unique blend of adventure and solitude. While this experience can be incredibly rewarding, it also comes with its set of challenges, particularly regarding safety. Being in the wilderness means being away from the convenience and security of urban areas, requiring careful preparation and awareness. This section explores essential tips for staying safe in the wilderness during an RV trip, focusing on preparedness, awareness, and respect for nature.

The first step towards ensuring safety in the wilderness is thorough preparation before embarking on the journey. This preparation involves researching the destination thoroughly, understanding the terrain, climate, potential hazards, and any wildlife you might encounter. It's also crucial to inform someone—a friend, family member, or park ranger—of your travel plans, including your route and expected return time. In case of any unforeseen circumstances, someone will know where to look for you.

When it comes to packing, it's essential to bring appropriate gear and supplies. This includes not only personal items but also safety equipment. A first-aid kit and items like a multi-tool, flashlight, extra batteries, a whistle, and a fire starter are necessary. Bear spray or other wildlife deterrents might be required depending on the area. It's also essential to pack appropriate clothing. Even in summer, temperatures can drop significantly at night, so layers of clothing, including a waterproof and windproof jacket, are advisable.

An understanding of your RV's capabilities and limitations is equally essential. Ensure your RV is in good condition before the trip, with all systems, including navigation, communication, and emergency features, functioning properly. Knowing how to perform basic repairs on your

RV can be invaluable, as professional help may not be readily available in remote areas.

Navigation skills are crucial in the wilderness. GPS devices are useful, but they can fail or lose signal in remote areas. Hence, carrying a detailed map of the area and a compass, and knowing how to use them, is vital. It's also essential to stay on designated trails and roads, as straying can lead to getting lost or inadvertently causing harm to protected ecosystems.

Water safety is another critical aspect. Always have a sufficient supply of water, and if you rely on natural sources, ensure you have a way to purify it, such as boiling, chemical purifiers, or a filtration system. Dehydration can be a serious risk, especially in hot or arid environments.

When it comes to food, proper storage and disposal are essential for your safety and to protect wildlife. In areas with bears and other wildlife, use bear-proof containers and dispose of trash in designated areas or take it with you when you leave. Keep food and trash securely stored away from your sleeping area.

Fire safety is paramount in the wilderness. If you plan to have a campfire, make sure it's permitted and always use designated fire rings. Never leave a fire unattended, and ensure it's completely extinguished before leaving the site or going to sleep. A small spark can lead to a catastrophic wildfire, especially in dry conditions.

Wildlife encounters can be one of the most thrilling aspects of wilderness camping but can pose significant risks. The key to safely coexisting with wildlife is to observe from a distance and never approach or feed animals. Understanding the behavior of local wildlife and how to respond in an encounter is crucial. For example, the way one should behave when encountering a bear is different from how one should act if facing a mountain lion.

Weather in the wilderness can be unpredictable, and sudden changes can pose serious risks. Stay updated on weather forecasts and be prepared for rapid changes. This might mean turning back during a hike if the weather worsens or seeking shelter during storms.

In case of emergencies, having a plan and the means to call for help is essential. While cell phones may not always have a signal in remote areas, devices like satellite phones or personal locator beacons can be lifesavers. Familiarize yourself with the procedure to seek help in the area you are visiting.
Lastly, practicing Leave No Trace principles ensures that the wilderness stays wild and unharmed by your visit. This includes minimizing campsite alterations, avoiding disturbing wildlife, packing out all trash, and leaving what you find.

In conclusion, staying safe in the wilderness during an RV trip requires a combination of preparation, awareness, and respect for nature. By understanding and preparing for the challenges of wilderness camping, travelers can enjoy the beauty and solitude of nature while minimizing risks. Whether navigating remote trails, observing wildlife, or simply enjoying the peace of the great outdoors, safety should always be a top priority. With careful planning and a respectful approach to the environment, an RV trip into the wilderness can be a safe, enjoyable, and unforgettable experience.

# CHAPTER VIII

# Wildlife Encounters and Safety

## Identifying and observing wildlife

RV camping provides an excellent opportunity to connect with nature and observe wildlife in its natural habitat. This experience of encountering wildlife is both exhilarating and educational, offering a deeper understanding and appreciation for the natural world. However, wildlife observation must be done responsibly to ensure the safety of both the animals and the observers. This section explores the intricacies of identifying and observing wildlife during RV camping, emphasizing the importance of preparation, ethical practices, and safety.

Preparation is a crucial aspect of wildlife observation.

Before embarking on an RV trip, it is beneficial to research the types of wildlife that are common in the destination area. Understanding the local ecosystems and the species they support can significantly enhance the wildlife watching experience. Resources such as field guides, wildlife identification apps, and local wildlife websites can provide valuable information on animal behavior, habitat, and identification tips. Familiarizing oneself with these resources beforehand can make wildlife identification more rewarding and accurate.

Equally important is bringing the right equipment for wildlife observation. Binoculars are essential for viewing animals from a safe and respectful distance. A good pair of binoculars can bring distant wildlife into clear view without approaching closely, which can disturb the animals. For those interested in bird watching, a field guide to birds of the region can be invaluable. Additionally, a camera with a zoom lens can capture wildlife sightings without encroaching on the animal's space.

Understanding and respecting wildlife behavior is crucial for safe and responsible observation. Human presence stresses or threatens animals, so maintaining a safe distance is essential. This distance varies depending on the species and the situation, but as a general rule, you are too close if the animal changes its behavior due to your presence. Observers should never attempt to feed, touch, or interact with wildlife, as this can disrupt their natural behaviors and potentially lead to dangerous encounters.

Timing can significantly enhance the wildlife observation experience. Many animals are most active during dawn and dusk, making these ideal times for observation. Additionally, understanding the seasonal behaviors of wildlife, such as migration patterns or breeding seasons, can lead to more fruitful wildlife watching opportunities. It's also beneficial to be patient and quiet while observing wildlife, as this increases the chances of seeing animals and not scaring them away.

Ethical practices are at the heart of responsible wildlife observation. This includes respecting the habitat of the animals and minimizing the impact of your presence. Staying on designated trails and roads, avoiding sensitive areas like nesting or denning sites, and not removing any natural materials are all essential practices. Wildlife should be allowed to remain wild, and any actions that could potentially habituate them to human presence should be avoided.

Safety is paramount when observing wildlife. While attacks on humans are rare, they can occur, particularly if animals feel threatened. Knowing how to react in the presence of potentially dangerous wildlife is essential. For example, in bear country, understanding bear behavior and knowing how to use bear spray can be life-saving. In general, never approach or corner wild animals; always have an escape route in mind.

In addition to observing wildlife from a distance, there are opportunities for close encounters at many campgrounds and national parks. Visitor centers often offer educational programs that include safe wildlife viewing. These programs can provide insightful information and a controlled environment for observing certain species.

Documenting wildlife sightings can also be a rewarding aspect of RV camping. Keeping a journal of the animals seen and details such as the location, time, and behavior observed can enhance the experience. This serves as a personal record and can be valuable for citizen science projects that track wildlife sightings.

Understanding the impact of human activity on wildlife is another crucial aspect of responsible observation. Noise pollution from vehicles, campgrounds, and outdoor activities can disturb wildlife. Reducing noise levels, keeping pets under control, and minimizing light pollution at night are all ways to reduce this impact.

Promoting conservation is an extension of wildlife observation. By appreciating wildlife and their habitats, RV campers can become advocates for conservation efforts. Supporting conservation organizations, participating in wildlife-friendly practices, and educating others about the importance of protecting wildlife can all contribute to the preservation of these species for future generations.

In conclusion, observing wildlife during RV camping offers a unique opportunity to connect with nature and learn about the diverse species that inhabit our natural landscapes. By preparing adequately, practicing ethical observation techniques, respecting wildlife and their habitats, and prioritizing safety, RV campers can enjoy the wonders of wildlife responsibly. This responsible approach not only ensures the safety and well-being of both wildlife and observers but also contributes to the broader goal of wildlife conservation. Through mindful and respectful wildlife observation, RV campers can play a role in preserving the beauty and diversity of nature for future generations to appreciate and enjoy.

## Safety guidelines for encounters with wild animals

RV trips offer the thrilling opportunity to explore and connect with nature. However, this adventure often brings travelers into close proximity with wild animals. While such encounters can be exhilarating, they also require a heightened awareness of safety. Respecting wildlife and understanding how to react during encounters is crucial for the safety of both the animals and the travelers. This section discusses comprehensive safety guidelines for encounters with wild animals during an RV trip.

Maintaining a respectful distance is the first and most fundamental rule in wildlife safety. Wildlife should be observed from afar to avoid disturbing their natural behaviors or causing them stress. Each species has a 'comfort zone,' and intruding into this space can provoke defensive behavior. For larger animals such as bears, moose, or elk, a safe distance is generally at least 100 yards. For smaller wildlife, a minimum of 30 yards is often recommended. Binoculars or zoom lenses on cameras can help in observing animals from these safe distances. Understanding animal behavior is key to staying safe.

Each species has unique behaviors and signs that indicate stress or aggression. For example, a bear might show its discomfort by huffing, stamping its feet, or making bluff charges. On the other hand, a mountain lion might hiss, crouch, or twitch its tail. Recognizing these signs can provide critical seconds to react appropriately.

In the event of an encounter with a potentially dangerous animal, such as a bear or a mountain lion, it's essential to know how to respond. If you encounter a bear, the general advice is to stay calm, speak in a low, calm voice, and slowly back away. Avoid running or making sudden movements, as this can trigger a predatory response. If the bear follows, stand your ground and make yourself appear larger. With mountain lions, maintain eye contact, make noise, and try to look intimidating. In the unlikely event of an attack, fight back vigorously.

Carrying and knowing how to use bear spray can be a lifesaver in bear country. Bear spray should be readily accessible, not buried in a backpack. However, it's crucial to understand its effective range and limitations, and only to use it as a last resort.

Storing food and scented items properly is crucial in wildlife territory. Animals have keen senses of smell and can be attracted to food, garbage, toiletries, and even aromatic candles. Use bear-proof containers or store such items in your RV. Never leave food or garbage outside unattended. This not only protects you but also prevents animals from becoming habituated to human food, which can ultimately endanger them.
If you're traveling with pets, keep them on a leash and under control. Free-roaming pets can attract wildlife and may not understand the danger they face from wild animals. Additionally, their presence can disturb local wildlife, disrupting natural behaviors and ecosystems.

Camping in areas known for wildlife requires additional precautions. When selecting a campsite, look for signs of recent wildlife activity such as tracks or scat. Avoid camping in areas that seem to be frequented by animals. Keeping a clean campsite is essential, as is cooking and eating away from your sleeping area.

Educating children about wildlife safety is also essential. They should understand the importance of keeping a safe distance from animals and what to do if they encounter wildlife. It's crucial to supervise children closely in areas where wildlife is present.

Another essential aspect of wildlife safety is knowing the local regulations and guidelines. National parks and wilderness areas often have specific rules regarding wildlife interactions. These can include restrictions on feeding animals, guidelines on safe viewing distances, and areas that are off-limits due to high wildlife activity. In case of an injury or dangerous encounter, having a plan for emergency communication is essential. Cell phone coverage can be unreliable in remote areas, so consider alternative communication methods like satellite phones or personal locator beacons. Knowing the location of the nearest ranger station or emergency facility is also wise. Lastly, remember that every wild animal encounter is unique, and there is no one-size-fits-all response. Staying informed, being aware of your surroundings, and using common sense are your best tools. Reading recent reports of wildlife activity in the area you're visiting can provide valuable insights into what to expect and how to prepare.

In conclusion, encountering wild animals is a significant part of the RV experience, offering a unique connection with nature. However, it comes with the responsibility of ensuring personal safety and the well-being of the wildlife. By maintaining a respectful distance, understanding animal behavior, storing food properly, and preparing for emergencies, RV travelers can safely enjoy the wonders of wildlife. These guidelines not only protect individuals but also contribute to the conservation of the very animals they admire, ensuring that these encounters remain a fascinating part of the wilderness experience for generations to come.

# Responsible wildlife photography

Wildlife photography during an RV trip combines the love for nature, travel, and the art of photography. It's an opportunity to capture the beauty and essence of wildlife in their natural habitat. However, this pursuit comes with a significant responsibility towards the wildlife and the environment. Responsible wildlife photography is not just about taking stunning pictures; it's about respecting the natural world and ensuring that our actions do not negatively impact the subjects we are capturing. This section explores the ethics, techniques, and considerations of responsible wildlife photography during an RV trip.

The first principle of responsible wildlife photography is to respect the wildlife and its habitat. This means maintaining a safe distance from the animals to avoid causing them stress or altering their natural behaviors. Many species are sensitive to human presence and can become agitated or frightened, which can lead to harmful situations for both the animal and the photographer. Using a zoom lens is an excellent way to capture close-up shots without intruding into the animal's space. Moreover, it's crucial to never bait or lure wildlife for the sake of a photo, as this can disrupt their natural foraging habits and make them accustomed to human interaction, potentially leading to dangerous encounters.

Understanding the wildlife you are photographing is vital. This involves researching their behavior, habitat, and needs. Knowing how to interpret an animal's behavior can help in recognizing signs of distress or agitation. For instance, birds fluttering away or mammals turning away might indicate that they feel threatened. A responsible photographer is always prepared to back off if their presence is causing disturbance.

Timing and patience are key components of wildlife photography. Animals are most active during the early mornings and late evenings, which are also the times when the natural light is most favorable for photography. This requires patience and often, long waits to capture the perfect shot. Responsible photographers understand that not every outing will result in spectacular photos, but the experience of being in nature and observing wildlife is rewarding in itself.

The importance of staying on designated trails and respecting restricted areas cannot be overstated. While the temptation to venture off the path for a unique shot might be strong, doing so can damage fragile habitats and disturb wildlife. Sticking to trails and observation points ensures that the natural environment is preserved, and wildlife is not unduly impacted by human presence.

Responsible wildlife photographers also practice ethical editing and sharing of images. This means being truthful about the circumstances in which the photo was taken and avoiding sensationalism. Manipulating images to create misleading impressions about wildlife behaviors or habitats can spread misinformation and potentially harm conservation efforts.

Noise disturbance is another aspect to consider. Keeping noise to a minimum is crucial, as loud sounds can startle wildlife, causing them unnecessary stress. This is especially important when photographing species that are sensitive to disturbance, such as nesting birds or reclusive mammals.

In the context of an RV trip, photographers should also be mindful of their vehicle. RVs should be parked in designated areas to avoid damaging natural habitats. Turning off the engine and lights when waiting for wildlife reduces noise and light disturbance and minimizes the environmental impact.

The role of wildlife photography in conservation should not be underestimated. Photographs can play a powerful role in raising awareness about wildlife and the challenges they face. Responsible photographers can use their images to educate and inspire others about the importance of conservation and respect for nature.

Safety is a priority, not just for the wildlife, but for the photographer as well. Wild animals are unpredictable, and it's essential to always be aware of your surroundings and prepared for unexpected situations. This includes knowing how to respond in case of an encounter with potentially dangerous wildlife and having a first-aid kit and communication equipment in case of emergencies.

Finally, it's essential to reflect on the purpose and impact of your photography. The goal should be celebrating wildlife and encouraging others to respect and protect the natural world. Responsible wildlife photography is about creating a connection between the viewer and the subject, fostering a sense of wonder and a desire to preserve the beauty of nature.

In conclusion, responsible wildlife photography during an RV trip is a practice that demands respect for nature, ethical behavior, and a commitment to conservation. It's about capturing the beauty of wildlife without causing harm or distress, understanding animal behavior, and appreciating the patience and skill required to photograph them in their natural environments. By adhering to these principles, wildlife photographers can enjoy their passion while contributing positively to the well-being of the natural world. The images captured can become visually stunning artworks and powerful tools for promoting awareness and conservation of the incredible wildlife that shares our planet.

# CHAPTER IX

# Connecting with Nature

## Mindfulness and meditation in nature

Recreational vehicle (RV) trips offer a unique opportunity to escape the hustle and bustle of daily life and immerse oneself in the tranquility of nature. This setting is perfect for practicing mindfulness and meditation, activities that can significantly enhance the RV experience. Engaging in mindfulness and meditation amidst natural surroundings not only provides relaxation and stress relief but also fosters a deeper connection with the environment. This section explores the integration of mindfulness and meditation into an RV trip, highlighting their benefits and offering practical tips for a fulfilling practice.

At its core, mindfulness is the practice of being fully present and engaged in the moment, with a gentle and accepting attitude. In the context of an RV trip, it means consciously experiencing the journey and the environment with all your senses. It could be as simple as savoring the sun's warmth, listening to the rustle of leaves, or watching the stars in the night sky. Mindfulness can transform ordinary activities like hiking, bird watching, or sitting by a campfire into deeply enriching experiences.

Meditation, often paired with mindfulness, involves techniques to focus and quiet the mind, often leading to a state of deep peace and relaxation. Meditation can take on a new dimension in the natural settings often sought out in RV trips. The serene environment enhances the practice, creating a more profound sense of peace and connection with nature.

To incorporate mindfulness and meditation into your RV trip, create a conducive environment. Find a quiet spot where you can sit or lie comfortably without interruptions. This could be a secluded area near your campsite, a peaceful lakeshore, or even a quiet corner inside your RV. The key is to be in a space where you feel relaxed and at ease.

Set aside dedicated time for your practice. Early mornings or evenings are often ideal as they offer a natural sense of calm and are typically quieter. However, the best time is one that fits seamlessly into your travel schedule. Even a few minutes of mindfulness or meditation can be beneficial, so don't feel pressured to allocate a large chunk of time.

When practicing mindfulness, engage your senses fully. Pay attention to the sights, sounds, and smells around you. Notice the colors of the sky, the patterns of leaves, the feel of the breeze. This sensory awareness grounds you in the present moment and enhances your connection to nature.

In meditation, focus on your breath or use guided meditations, which can be particularly helpful for beginners. The sound of a flowing stream, the sight of a mountain range, or even the rhythm of your breathing can serve as focal points for meditation. The idea is to gently bring your attention back to these points whenever your mind wanders.

One of the benefits of mindfulness and meditation during an RV trip is the reduction of stress. The combination of these practices with the natural calm of the outdoors can have a powerful effect on your mental well-being, helping to soothe anxiety and promote a sense of inner peace.

Practicing mindfulness and meditation also enhances your appreciation of the natural world. By slowing down and observing nature attentively, you develop a more profound respect and connection to the environment. This heightened appreciation can transform how you experience your RV trip, turning ordinary moments into extraordinary ones.

Mindfulness and meditation can also improve the quality of your interactions with fellow travelers. By cultivating a calm and present state of mind, you may enhance your patience, empathy, and communication skills, leading to more meaningful and harmonious relationships.

Incorporating mindfulness and meditation into hiking, fishing, or bird watching activities can enrich these experiences. For instance, mindful walking involves being fully present with each step, feeling the ground beneath your feet, and observing your surroundings without judgment. This can transform a simple hike into a profoundly grounding and rejuvenating experience.

Journaling can be a valuable tool in your mindfulness practice. Writing about your experiences, thoughts, and feelings helps process them and deepen your mindfulness practice. It also serves as a wonderful keepsake of your journey, capturing the essence of your RV trip in words.

Lastly, it's essential to approach mindfulness and meditation with a non-judgmental attitude. The goal is not to empty your mind of thoughts or achieve a state of bliss but to be present and aware. It's normal for the mind to wander; the practice lies in gently bringing your attention back to the present moment.

In conclusion, incorporating mindfulness and meditation into an RV trip can significantly enhance the experience. These practices provide a pathway to connect deeply with nature, reduce stress, and enjoy each moment to its fullest. Whether sitting quietly by a lake, meditating under the stars, or simply being fully present with the sights and sounds of the wilderness, mindfulness and meditation are powerful tools for enriching your journey. They transform an RV trip from a simple getaway into a profound experience of relaxation, rejuvenation, and connection with the natural world.

## Strategies for unplugging and disconnecting from technology

In today's digital age, disconnecting from technology can be challenging. An RV trip presents a unique opportunity to unplug from the constant buzz of screens and notifications, offering a chance to reconnect with nature and oneself. This disconnection, however, requires intentional strategies to ensure that the allure of technology does not overshadow the experience of the journey. This section explores various methods for effectively unplugging from technology during an RV trip, emphasizing the importance of preparation, mindset, and engagement with the natural world.

The journey towards unplugging begins well before the RV hits the road. Preparation is key, and this starts with setting clear intentions for the trip. It's important to define the purpose of disconnecting: to spend quality time with family, enjoy nature, or find personal relaxation. Understanding your 'why' helps in staying committed to the goal of unplugging.

Informing others of your intention to disconnect is also vital. Let friends, family, and work colleagues know that you will be less reachable, setting expectations for limited communication. This not only reduces the anxiety of missing out but also mitigates the pressure to check devices constantly.

Creating a tech-free zone in the RV can be a practical step towards minimizing digital distractions. Designate areas, such as the dining or sleeping areas, where electronic devices are not allowed. This helps create physical boundaries that reinforce your intention to disconnect.

However, completely eschewing technology might not be practical or safe, especially regarding navigation or emergency communication. The key is to use technology mindfully. Limit the use of devices to essential functions, such as GPS for directions or a quick check of weather updates. Avoid using devices for entertainment or habitual scrolling through social media.

Replacing screen time with alternative activities is crucial in successfully disconnecting. Plan activities that engage everyone and encourage outdoor engagement, like hiking, biking, or fishing. Evenings around the campfire can be filled with storytelling, stargazing, or playing musical instruments. The goal is to replace the passive consumption of digital content with active, enriching experiences.

Bringing books, journals, or board games can provide entertainment and relaxation without the need for screens. These activities help pass the time and encourage creativity, introspection, and bonding with fellow travelers.

Mindfulness practices can play a significant role in the disconnection process. Engage in activities like meditation, yoga, or mindful walking, focusing on being present. These practices help in grounding yourself in the experience of the trip, rather than being distracted by digital devices.

While often reliant on technology, photography can be approached as a mindful activity rather than a digital distraction. Use photography as a means to engage with your surroundings, capturing moments of beauty and interest. However, be mindful not to let the act of taking photos overshadow the experience of the moment itself.

Setting specific times to check devices, if necessary, can help manage the urge to be online constantly. For instance, allotting a short time in the morning or evening to check emails or messages can keep you connected to essential communication while avoiding constant digital engagement.

Engaging with nature is perhaps the most effective strategy for unplugging. The natural environment offers endless opportunities for exploration and appreciation. Activities like bird watching, identifying flora, or simply observing the landscapes can be deeply fulfilling experiences that do not require any form of technology. For families, encouraging children to disconnect can be particularly challenging. Involving them in planning and executing trip activities can keep them engaged and interested. Encourage them to keep a travel journal, collect natural souvenirs, or participate in outdoor games.

Reflecting on the experience of being unplugged is essential. This could involve discussing the day's experiences with travel companions, journaling, or simply contemplating. Reflection helps in recognizing the benefits of being disconnected and reinforces the decision to stay unplugged.
Finally, being flexible and patient with yourself and others is essential. The habit of constantly checking devices can be deeply ingrained, and it may take time to adjust to being unplugged. Recognize and celebrate the small successes in your journey towards disconnection.

In conclusion, disconnecting from technology during an RV trip is a process that requires intentional preparation, mindful engagement, and a commitment to exploring alternative activities. By setting clear intentions, creating tech-free zones, and immersing oneself in the richness of nature and mindful practices, it is possible to break free from the digital tether. This disconnection allows for a deeper connection with the natural world and fosters personal well-being and meaningful interactions with fellow travelers. An RV trip, free from the constant distraction of technology, can thus become a truly transformative experience, offering a much-needed respite in our digitally saturated lives.

## Benefits of connecting with the natural world

An RV trip presents a unique opportunity to escape the confines of urban life and immerse oneself in the natural world. This connection with nature is not just a mere change of scenery; it offers profound physical, mental, and emotional benefits. From the tranquil forests to the vast, open landscapes, nature provides an environment to unwind, rejuvenate, and gain a deeper appreciation for the world's natural wonders. This section delves into the multifaceted benefits of connecting with nature during an RV trip.

The first and perhaps most immediate benefit is reducing stress and anxiety. Natural environments have a calming effect on the mind. The sounds of a flowing river, the rustling of leaves in the wind, or the birds chirping at dawn all contribute to a sense of peace and tranquility. Studies have shown that spending time in nature decreases cortisol levels, a hormone associated with stress. This natural de-stressing starkly contrasts the often frenetic energy of city life, offering a chance for individuals to unwind and decompress.

Being in nature during an RV trip physically encourages a more active lifestyle. Whether hiking, swimming in a lake, or simply walking through a forest, these activities provide enjoyable and beneficial exercise to physical health. The natural terrain offers a more varied and stimulating environment for physical activity compared to the monotony of a treadmill or a gym. This improves physical fitness and contributes to better cardiovascular health, increased stamina, and enhanced immune system function.

The exposure to natural light is another significant benefit. In our daily lives, especially in urban settings, we are often subjected to artificial lighting, which can disrupt our natural circadian rhythms. Natural sunlight, particularly in the morning, helps regulate our internal body clock, improving sleep quality and overall mood. Moreover, sunlight is a vital source of Vitamin D, essential for bone health and immune function.

Connecting with nature also has profound psychological benefits. It allows for introspection and self-reflection, away from the distractions and demands of everyday life. Nature's inherent beauty and simplicity can inspire feelings of awe and wonder, leading to a more profound sense of well-being. This connection often leads to a contemplative state, where one can ponder life's more significant questions, reassess priorities, and gain clarity on personal goals and aspirations.

For families, an RV trip in nature provides a unique opportunity for bonding and shared experiences. Apart from the constant pull of screens and technology, families can engage in activities fostering cooperation, communication, and deeper connections. Shared experiences like setting up camp, cooking meals over a fire, or exploring a trail can strengthen relationships and create lasting memories.

The educational aspect of being in nature is particularly beneficial for children. It offers a hands-on learning experience where children can learn about different ecosystems, wildlife, and plants. This interaction with the natural world can foster curiosity, creativity, and a love for learning that extends beyond the confines of a traditional classroom.

From an environmental perspective, spending time in nature can foster a deeper understanding and appreciation for the environment. This connection often leads to a heightened awareness of environmental issues and a more profound commitment to sustainable living practices. When people experience the beauty and fragility of natural environments firsthand, they are more likely to advocate for conservation efforts and be mindful of their ecological footprint.

Being in nature also provides therapeutic benefits, often called ecotherapy or nature therapy. This form of therapy has been shown to be effective in reducing symptoms of depression, anxiety, and other mental health conditions. The therapeutic effect of natural environments can be attributed to their ability to provide a sense of calm, a break from stimulus overload, and a feeling of being grounded in a larger, living system.

Moreover, nature provides a canvas for artistic inspiration. Many artists, writers, and musicians find that being in natural settings stimulates their creativity. The colors of a sunset, the patterns of leaves, or the sound of waves can all inspire artistic expression. For those creatively inclined, an RV trip can be a discovery and artistic rejuvenation journey.

Finally, the simplicity of life on an RV trip can lead to a greater sense of gratitude and contentment. Away from the materialistic and consumer-driven culture, one can find joy in simple pleasures – a quiet evening by the campfire, the beauty of a starry sky, or the fresh scent of a forest after rain. This simplicity can lead to a more mindful approach to life, where one learns to appreciate the present moment and the simple joys it offers.

In conclusion, connecting with the natural world during an RV trip offers many benefits that encompass physical, mental, and emotional well-being. It provides an escape from the stresses of daily life, encourages physical activity, and offers a space for introspection and creativity. It strengthens family bonds, fosters environmental stewardship, and provides a platform for education and personal growth. An RV trip into nature is not just a getaway; it's an opportunity to rediscover and reconnect with the fundamental aspects of life that bring true joy and fulfillment.

# CHAPTER X

# Eco-Friendly RV Camping

## Sustainable RV practices

In the realm of recreational vehicle (RV) camping, sustainability has become an increasingly important topic. As more people seek the freedom and adventure that comes with RV travel, there is a growing recognition of the need to minimize the environmental impact of such activities. Sustainable RV practices encompass a range of strategies and actions to reduce the ecological footprint of camping and traveling in an RV. This section delves into these practices, exploring how RV enthusiasts can enjoy the wonders of mobile living in an environmentally responsible manner.

The concept of sustainability in RV camping is multifaceted, touching upon aspects such as energy usage, waste management, water conservation, and the overall environmental impact of RVs. One of the primary concerns is the carbon footprint associated with driving large, often less fuel-efficient vehicles. To address this, RVers can adopt practices that improve fuel efficiency, such as regular maintenance checks to ensure the RV is running smoothly, driving at optimal speeds to reduce fuel consumption, and planning routes efficiently to minimize unnecessary travel. Additionally, the advent of more eco-friendly RV models, including those powered by alternative fuels or hybrid technologies, offers promising avenues for reducing emissions.

Energy consumption is another critical area for sustainable RV practices. Traditional RVs rely heavily on generators and external power sources, which can have significant environmental impacts. Transitioning to renewable energy sources, such as installing solar panels, can be a game-changer. Solar energy can power lights, appliances, and electronic devices, reducing reliance on non-renewable energy sources and cutting down on generator noise and emissions. LED lighting and energy-efficient appliances further contribute to reducing energy consumption.

Water conservation is especially crucial in RV camping, as water is a finite and essential resource. Simple changes like installing low-flow faucets and showerheads, fixing leaks promptly, and using water-saving practices such as turning off the tap while brushing teeth can make a substantial difference. Additionally, mindful usage of cleaning products and soaps that are biodegradable and eco-friendly helps protect the environment from harmful chemicals.

Waste management is a significant aspect of sustainable RV living. Proper disposal of waste, including separating recyclables and avoiding single-use plastics, is essential. Composting organic waste is an excellent way to reduce the amount of trash heading to landfills and can provide nutrient-rich material for soil. Moreover, responsible RVers should always adhere to the principles of Leave No Trace, ensuring that they leave their camping spots as pristine as they found them, if not more so.

Beyond these practical measures, sustainable RV practices also encompass a broader ethos of environmental stewardship. This includes being mindful of the natural habitats and wildlife in the areas visited. Sticking to established trails, avoiding the disturbance of flora and fauna, and respecting any local conservation efforts are all part of this responsible approach.

Engaging with local communities is another dimension of sustainable RVing. Supporting local businesses, buying local produce, and participating in community-led environmental initiatives can enhance the RVing experience and contribute to the economic and ecological well-being of the places visited. This approach fosters a sense of connection and responsibility towards the local environments and communities.

Another important consideration is the choice of camping locations. Opting for eco-friendly campgrounds that employ sustainable practices such as renewable energy, water conservation measures, and recycling programs can significantly reduce the environmental impact of RV camping. Some campgrounds are specifically designed with sustainability in mind, offering facilities that align with eco-friendly living.

Education and awareness are crucial components of sustainable RV practices. Staying informed about environmental issues, understanding the impact of one's actions, and learning about sustainable practices are ongoing processes. RVers can share knowledge and experiences with the community, promoting a culture of sustainability within the RVing world. This can include participating in workshops, joining online forums, and engaging with environmental organizations.

Adopting a minimalist and mindful approach to RV living can also contribute to sustainability. This involves carefully considering what to pack and bring along, focusing on essentials and multi-use items, and avoiding the accumulation of unnecessary goods and possessions. A minimalist approach not only reduces waste and consumption but also aligns with the freedom and simplicity that many seek in RV travel.

Finally, sustainable RVing also means being prepared for emergencies in an environmentally conscious way. This includes having eco-friendly emergency supplies, understanding how to deal with wildlife encounters responsibly, and knowing how to minimize one's impact while dealing with unexpected situations.

In conclusion, sustainable RV practices are about harmonizing the love for travel and adventure with a deep respect for the environment. By adopting measures to reduce emissions, conserve energy and water, manage waste responsibly, and engage with local communities, RVers can significantly diminish their ecological footprint. The essence of sustainable RVing lies in recognizing that the natural world is a shared and precious resource that requires our care and protection. Through mindful actions and a commitment to sustainability, the RV community can ensure that the joys of RV camping are preserved for future generations to enjoy and cherish.

## Reducing your carbon footprint while camping

Camping with a recreational vehicle (RV) offers a unique experience of exploration and adventure. However, this mode of travel can considerably impact the environment, primarily through its carbon footprint. The carbon footprint of RV camping comes from various sources, including vehicle emissions, energy use, and waste generation. Reducing this footprint is an essential step towards more sustainable travel. This section explores several strategies to minimize the carbon footprint while camping with an RV, covering aspects such as fuel efficiency, energy conservation, waste reduction, and eco-friendly habits.

The journey towards a lower carbon footprint in RV camping begins with the vehicle itself. Fuel consumption is a major contributor to carbon emissions. To mitigate this, selecting an appropriately sized RV for your needs and more fuel-efficient is a crucial first step. Modern RVs are being designed with better fuel efficiency and lower emissions in mind. Considering alternatives such as diesel engines, which can be more efficient than gasoline engines, or even exploring hybrid or electric RV options, can significantly impact reducing emissions.

Once on the road, driving habits also play a crucial role in fuel consumption. Maintaining a steady speed, avoiding rapid acceleration and heavy braking, and properly planning routes to avoid unnecessary mileage can enhance fuel efficiency. Regular RV maintenance, including checking tire pressure, changing oil, and ensuring the engine runs smoothly, further optimizes fuel use.

The use of energy within the RV is another area where significant reductions in carbon footprint can be achieved. Incorporating renewable energy sources can reduce reliance on generators and hookups. Installing solar panels on the RV is a practical solution that provides a clean and renewable source of power. Solar energy can be used for lighting, charging electronics, and powering appliances, thereby reducing reliance on non-renewable energy sources.

In addition to solar power, upgrading to energy-efficient appliances and lighting can drastically reduce energy consumption. LED lights, energy-efficient refrigerators, and other low-energy appliances are not only better for the environment but also reduce the strain on the RV's electrical system. Smart energy use, such as turning off lights and appliances when not in use and optimizing natural light during the day, further conserves energy.

Water conservation is another important aspect of reducing the carbon footprint in RV camping. Efficient use of water resources minimizes the need for energy-intensive water pumping and heating. Installing low-flow faucets and showerheads, fixing leaks promptly, and using water-saving practices like turning off the tap while brushing teeth can significantly reduce water usage. Additionally, using biodegradable soaps and cleaning products ensures that greywater disposal has a minimal environmental impact.

Waste management is crucial in reducing the environmental impact of RV camping. Minimizing waste production, particularly of single-use plastics, is the first step. Bringing reusable containers, utensils, and bags, and buying products with minimal packaging can significantly cut down waste. Properly sorting and disposing of waste, recycling whenever possible, and composting organic waste are practices that reduce carbon footprint.

Another strategy for reducing emissions is to spend more time in each location rather than moving frequently. This not only cuts down on fuel consumption but also allows for a deeper exploration and appreciation of each destination. Staying longer in one place can also encourage a more relaxed and mindful camping experience.

Food choices and cooking methods also contribute to the carbon footprint of RV camping. Opting for locally sourced and organic food reduces the emissions associated with food transportation and production. Cooking methods requiring less energy, such as grilling outdoors or using a solar oven, are more eco-friendly than traditional stovetop or oven cooking.

The choice of camping location can also influence the carbon footprint. Choosing campgrounds that implement sustainable practices, such as renewable energy, water conservation measures, and recycling programs, supports a more sustainable camping industry. Additionally, camping in locations closer to home reduces travel distance, thereby lowering fuel consumption and emissions.

Engaging in eco-friendly camping activities, such as hiking, biking, kayaking, or bird watching, provides entertainment and exercise with minimal environmental impact. These activities not only reduce reliance on motorized transportation but also foster a deeper connection with the natural environment.

Finally, educating oneself and advocating for sustainable practices is essential to reducing one's carbon footprint. Sharing knowledge and experiences with fellow campers, participating in environmental conservation initiatives, and supporting policies and practices that promote sustainability in the RV and camping industry contribute to a broader cultural shift towards more environmentally responsible travel.

In conclusion, reducing the carbon footprint while camping with an RV requires a multi-faceted approach encompassing mindful vehicle use, energy conservation, waste reduction, and sustainable living practices. By adopting these strategies, RV campers can significantly mitigate their environmental impact, ensuring that the natural beauty and resources we enjoy today are preserved for future generations. Embracing sustainable RV practices enhances the camping experience and contributes to the broader effort of protecting our planet.


## Preserving the beauty of national parks for future generations

National parks are often regarded as one of the greatest treasures of a nation, embodying the unspoiled beauty of nature and serving as sanctuaries for diverse wildlife and ecosystems. As these pristine areas face increasing pressures from environmental changes and human activities, the responsibility to preserve their beauty for future generations becomes more pressing. This section delves into the various strategies and practices necessary to protect and maintain the integrity of national parks, focusing on conservation efforts, responsible tourism, educational outreach, and community involvement.

Conservation efforts form the backbone of preserving national parks. These efforts involve a range of activities to protect the natural landscapes, flora, fauna, and the overall ecological balance of these parks. Conservation initiatives often require collaborative approaches involving government agencies, non-profit organizations, scientists, and local communities. Key activities include habitat restoration, wildlife conservation programs, scientific research on biodiversity and ecosystem health, and efforts to combat environmental threats such as pollution, climate change, invasive species, and illegal activities like poaching and deforestation.

Responsible tourism plays a pivotal role in the preservation of national parks. As visitor numbers continue to rise, the potential for environmental degradation increases. Implementing the 'Leave No Trace' principles is crucial to mitigate this. These principles guide visitors to minimize their environmental impact by staying on designated trails, disposing of waste properly, and respecting wildlife and their habitats. Additionally, park authorities can implement measures such as visitor education programs, regulated access to sensitive areas, and infrastructural developments like boardwalks and viewing platforms to minimize human impact.

Educating visitors about the significance of national parks is vital. Awareness and understanding of the unique ecosystems, their challenges, and the importance of conservation can significantly enhance visitor behavior. Educational initiatives can take many forms, such as interpretive trails, visitor center exhibits, guided tours, and ranger talks. These programs not only impart knowledge but also inspire a deeper appreciation and respect for the natural world, encouraging visitors to adopt sustainable practices both within and beyond the parks.

Local communities living near national parks play a crucial role in their preservation. Engaging these communities in the management and conservation of parks ensures that preservation efforts are inclusive and consider local needs and knowledge. This includes community-based conservation programs, sustainable tourism initiatives, and educational outreach. Involving local communities in decision-making processes can lead to more effective conservation strategies that benefit both the environment and the local populace.

Sustainable infrastructure development within national parks is essential for accommodating visitors without harming the environment. This includes eco-friendly facilities, waste management systems, and sustainable transportation options. Renewable energy sources, such as solar and wind power, can be utilized to power park facilities, reducing the parks' carbon footprint.

Continuous monitoring and research are key components in the preservation of national parks. Regular monitoring of wildlife populations, vegetation health, and ecological changes helps understand the impacts of environmental stressors and human activities. Scientific research can inform management decisions and conservation strategies, ensuring they are based on sound ecological principles.

Climate change poses a significant challenge to national parks, impacting ecosystems, biodiversity, and landscape features. Addressing this challenge involves both mitigating the effects of climate change within the parks and contributing to broader efforts to reduce greenhouse gas emissions. Enhancing the parks' resilience to climate impacts and integrating climate considerations into all aspects of park management are essential.

Volunteerism offers individuals a hands-on opportunity to contribute to preserving national parks. Many parks have volunteer programs that allow people to participate in conservation projects, visitor education, and park maintenance. These programs provide invaluable assistance to the parks and foster a personal connection to these natural areas.

Advocacy and public support are critical for the long-term preservation of national parks. Advocacy efforts can support policies and funding that bolster conservation efforts and expanding protected areas. Public support can also counteract proposed activities and developments that threaten the integrity of these natural areas.

Fostering a culture of respect and appreciation for nature in society at large is essential for the future preservation of national parks. Promoting environmental stewardship in educational institutions, encouraging media coverage of conservation issues, and celebrating the intrinsic value of natural environments are ways to cultivate this culture. A society that values and respects nature is more likely to support efforts to preserve its beauty and integrity.

In conclusion, preserving the beauty of national parks for future generations is a multifaceted endeavor that requires concerted efforts from all sectors of society. It involves conservation, responsible tourism, education, community engagement, sustainable development, and advocacy. By adopting these practices, we ensure that the wonders and beauty of our national parks endure, offering inspiration and enjoyment to countless future generations. These efforts protect these precious areas and contribute to a broader understanding and appreciation of the natural world, fostering a global commitment to its preservation.

# CHAPTER XI

# Troubleshooting and Common Challenges

## Dealing with common RV issues

Recreational vehicles (RVs) embody the spirit of adventure and the comfort of home, making them a popular choice for travel enthusiasts. However, like any vehicle or home, they are not immune to issues. Common RV problems range from mechanical failures to everyday living challenges within a confined space. Addressing these issues effectively is key to ensuring a smooth and enjoyable RV experience. This section explores various common RV issues and offers insights into how to handle them effectively.

One of the primary concerns for RV owners is mechanical reliability. Given that an RV is both a vehicle and a living space, mechanical issues can range from engine problems to faults in the onboard systems like plumbing and electrical. Regular maintenance is the first line of defense against mechanical failures. This includes routine engine, brakes, tires, and batteries checks. Engine problems are often the most disruptive, so ensuring the oil is regularly changed, filters are clean, and fluids are at the correct levels is crucial. Brakes should be inspected for wear, especially considering the additional weight they handle in an RV. Tires are another critical component; they should be checked for proper inflation, tread wear, and signs of damage before every trip.

Electrical issues in an RV can manifest in various ways, from malfunctioning lights to problems with the onboard generator. A typical electrical issue is battery failure, which can often be prevented by regular inspection and charging. RVs usually have separate batteries for the engine and the living quarters; both need regular checking. Electrical connections should be kept clean and tight, and fuses should be checked and replaced as necessary. If the RV has a generator, it should be run regularly to keep it in good working condition.

Plumbing issues are another common concern in RVs, including leaks, clogged pipes, and problems with the onboard toilet. Preventative measures include regular checks of all connections and using RV-specific chemicals to break down waste and prevent clogs in the sewage system. Leaks can often be fixed with simple tools and replacement parts, but more serious plumbing issues may require professional assistance.

The confined living space in an RV can also present challenges, particularly in terms of storage and organization. Efficient use of space is key, and this often requires creative solutions such as multi-purpose furniture, collapsible items, and maximizing vertical space with shelving and hooks. Keeping the RV organized makes living more comfortable and ensures safety, as loose items can become hazardous in transit.

Temperature control within an RV is essential for comfort. Insulation is key to maintaining a stable temperature, and windows can be a significant heat loss or gain source. Upgrading to double-pane windows, using thermal curtains, and ensuring all seals and weather-stripping are in good condition can help maintain the desired temperature. Air conditioning units and heaters should be serviced regularly to ensure they are operating efficiently.

Connectivity issues are a modern concern for many RV travelers, especially those who work on the road or value staying in touch with family and friends. While many campgrounds offer Wi-Fi, the service can be unreliable or slow. Solutions include investing in a good-quality mobile hotspot, using a signal booster, or seeking out campgrounds with better connectivity options.

Safety in an RV is paramount, extending beyond driving safety to include living safety. Smoke and carbon monoxide detectors should be installed and tested regularly. A fire extinguisher should be readily accessible, and all travelers should be aware of basic fire safety practices and the RV's emergency exits.

Food storage and preparation in an RV's compact kitchen present their own set of challenges. Efficient use of space, careful meal planning, and the use of compact appliances can make cooking and food storage more accessible. It's essential to understand the limitations of an RV refrigerator and pantry, plan meals accordingly, and make use of local produce and markets.

Water conservation is a significant aspect of RV living, especially when dry camping without hookups. Conserving water can be achieved by taking shorter showers, using a water-saving showerhead, and turning off the tap while brushing teeth or washing dishes. Monitoring water levels and understanding the capacity of your freshwater tank is also essential.

Finally, dealing with common RV issues often requires a level of self-sufficiency and a willingness to learn new skills. Carrying a basic tool kit, spare parts, and instructional manuals can enable RV owners to address minor repairs and issues themselves. For more complex problems, having a reliable RV repair service contact is essential.

In conclusion, owning and traveling in an RV can be an enriching experience, but it comes with its set of challenges. From mechanical and electrical issues to space management and safety concerns, being prepared and knowledgeable is vital. Regular maintenance, proactive problem-solving, and efficient use of space can help mitigate many common RV issues, ensuring a safe and comfortable journey. With some preparation and adaptability, RV enthusiasts can confidently handle the challenges of RV living, making the most of their adventures on the open road.

## Handling emergencies in the wilderness

RV camping in the wilderness offers a serene escape from the bustling city life, bringing you closer to nature's tranquility. However, this escape into the wild also comes with its unique set of challenges, particularly when it comes to emergencies. Being in a remote location can mean limited access to immediate help, making it essential to be prepared for various potential emergencies. This section explores how to handle emergencies during wilderness RV camping effectively, encompassing preparation, response strategies, and critical thinking.

Preparation is the cornerstone of handling emergencies effectively. Planning and preparing before embarking on an RV trip is crucial. This involves researching the area you will be visiting, including its wildlife, climate, and potential hazards. It's also important to inform someone about your travel plans, including your route and expected return time, so rescuers have a starting point in case of an emergency. Equipping your RV with essential emergency supplies such as a comprehensive first aid kit, emergency food and water, a reliable means of communication (like a satellite phone or a personal locator beacon), and essential survival gear is crucial. Understanding the workings of your RV is also part of being prepared. You should know your RV's electrical, plumbing, and heating systems. Knowing how to shut off gas and water supplies, how to troubleshoot fundamental mechanical issues, and what to do in case of an RV breakdown are vital skills. Keep a manual of your RV handy for quick reference in emergencies.

Navigational skills are key in wilderness camping. Despite the convenience of GPS devices, they can fail or lose signal in remote areas. A detailed map of the area and a compass are essential tools, and knowing how to use them effectively can be lifesaving if you get lost or need to guide rescuers to your location.

In case of a medical emergency, having basic first aid knowledge is invaluable. This includes knowing how to treat common injuries like cuts, burns, and sprains, recognizing symptoms of serious conditions like hypothermia or heatstroke, and understanding when to seek immediate help. Keep your first aid kit well-stocked and within easy reach.

Weather-related emergencies are a significant risk in the wilderness. Sudden changes in weather can lead to dangerous situations like flash floods, lightning storms, or blizzards. Awareness of the weather forecast and understanding how to seek shelter or secure your RV in adverse conditions is crucial. Always have a contingency plan in case the weather changes unexpectedly.

Encounters with wildlife can also pose emergencies. While wildlife attacks are rare, knowing how to coexist safely with animals you might encounter is important. This means storing food securely, disposing of waste properly, and understanding what to do if you encounter potentially dangerous wildlife. For example, knowing how to use bear spray in areas with bear activity can be a lifesaver.

Fire safety is paramount in the wilderness. When building a campfire, do so in designated areas, keep it controlled, and fully extinguish it before leaving or sleeping. Be extra cautious during dry seasons or in areas with high fire risk to prevent wildfires.

Mechanical failures in your RV can turn into emergencies in remote locations. Regular RV maintenance can prevent many issues, but preparing for breakdowns is also important. This includes having basic tools, knowing simple repairs, and having a plan for how to get help. Keep emergency roadside assistance contact information handy.

Dealing with emergencies also involves maintaining a calm and level-headed approach. In any emergency situation, assess the situation calmly, consider your options, and make informed decisions. If you are unsure, seek help or advice from authorities such as park rangers or emergency services.

Water emergencies can occur if you are camping near a body of water. Understanding water safety, including the risks of flooding or fast-moving water, is essential. Always set up camp at a safe distance from the water, especially if rain is forecasted, and ensure everyone knows basic water safety rules.

Finally, being prepared for emergencies in the wilderness also means being ready for extended stays. If an emergency prevents you from leaving as planned, having extra food, water, and medication supplies is essential. It's also important to have a way to communicate or signal for help if you are stranded.

In conclusion, handling emergencies in the wilderness during RV camping requires a combination of thorough preparation, practical knowledge, and a calm approach. By being well-prepared with the right equipment and knowledge, understanding how to respond to different types of emergencies, and maintaining a level head, RV campers can navigate through challenging situations and ensure their safety and the safety of their companions.

Whether it's addressing medical issues, weather-related challenges, wildlife encounters, or mechanical failures, effectively handling emergencies is an essential part of safe and responsible RV camping in the wilderness.

## Tips for staying safe and comfortable

RV camping combines the freedom of the road with the comforts of home, offering a unique way to explore and enjoy the outdoors. However, ensuring safety and comfort during an RV trip requires careful consideration and preparation. From maintaining the vehicle to creating a cozy living environment, numerous factors must be considered. This section provides a comprehensive guide to staying safe and comfortable during RV camping, covering vehicle maintenance, campsite setup, personal safety, and living comfort.

The foundation of a safe and comfortable RV trip is a well-maintained vehicle. Before embarking on any journey, conducting a thorough check of the RV is essential. This includes inspecting the engine, brakes, tires, and all electrical systems. Regular maintenance, such as oil changes, brake checks, and tire inspections, should be part of your routine before and during your trip. Ensuring that your RV is mechanically sound prevents breakdowns and ensures your safety on the road.

Tire maintenance deserves special attention, as tire issues are one of the most common causes of RV breakdowns. Check the tire pressure regularly, and make sure they are inflated to the manufacturer's recommended level. Inspect the tires for any signs of wear, cracks, or damage, and replace them if needed. Also, be sure to have a spare tire, jack, and the necessary tools to change a tire.

Due to its size and weight, driving an RV requires different skills than driving a regular vehicle. Familiarize yourself with the RV's dimensions and practice driving it in a variety of conditions. Pay special attention to height restrictions, especially when driving under bridges or through tunnels. While on the road, drive at a safe speed, and allow for extra stopping distance. Be aware of the weather conditions and adjust your driving accordingly.

When selecting a campsite, consider both safety and comfort. Choose a level spot to ensure that your RV is stable and that appliances, such as your refrigerator, operate correctly. Avoid parking under dead or weak branches, and be aware of your surroundings, including any wildlife activity. Check for any campground rules and regulations, and adhere to them for a safe and enjoyable experience.

Setting up your campsite is another important aspect of your safety and comfort. Level your RV using leveling blocks or jacks, and secure it with wheel chocks. Connect to utilities carefully, following safety guidelines, especially when dealing with electricity and water. Set up your living space outside the RV, such as chairs, tables, and awnings, to create a comfortable outdoor area.

Fire safety is crucial in RV camping. Equip your RV with smoke detectors, carbon monoxide detectors, and a fire extinguisher. Check them regularly to ensure they are functioning correctly. If you plan to have a campfire, do so responsibly. Use designated fire pits, control the fire, and never leave it unattended. Fully extinguish the fire before going to bed or leaving the campsite.

Food storage and preparation are important for both safety and comfort. Store perishable items in the refrigerator or a cooler to prevent spoilage. Be cautious when cooking inside the RV, as confined spaces can pose a fire risk. Ensure proper ventilation when using the stove, and never leave cooking unattended. Dispose of food waste properly to avoid attracting wildlife.

Personal safety should not be overlooked. Keep your RV locked when you're away, and be cautious about sharing your travel plans with strangers. Familiarize yourself with the emergency procedures of the campground and know the location of the nearest medical facilities. If traveling in remote areas, consider carrying a means of communication, such as a satellite phone or a personal locator beacon.

Water conservation is another aspect of comfortable RV camping, especially when dry camping without hookups. Use water-saving practices such as taking shorter showers, turning off the tap while brushing teeth, and using a spray nozzle on hoses. Installing water-saving devices like low-flow showerheads and faucets can also help conserve water.

Temperature control within the RV is key to comfort. Use window shades and awnings to keep the RV cool during hot weather, and consider using fans to circulate air. In colder weather, ensure that your RV's heating system is in good working order and consider using insulated curtains to keep the heat in. Always ensure proper ventilation to prevent condensation and maintain good air quality.

Maintaining cleanliness and hygiene in the confined space of an RV is essential. Regularly clean the interior, including the kitchen and bathroom areas, to prevent the buildup of dirt and germs. Organize your space to prevent clutter and create a more comfortable living environment.

Finally, staying connected can be important for many RV campers. While the idea of disconnecting from technology is appealing to some, others may need to stay in touch for work or personal reasons. Use a reliable cell phone provider, consider investing in a Wi-Fi booster, or plan your trip around locations with good connectivity.

In conclusion, staying safe and comfortable during an RV camping trip involves a mix of careful preparation, practical knowledge, and attention to personal well-being. By maintaining the RV, practicing safe driving, setting up a secure and cozy campsite, managing food and water resources wisely, and staying connected when necessary, RV campers can enjoy a fulfilling and comfortable outdoor experience. These practices ensure the safety and comfort of the travelers and contribute to a respectful and responsible enjoyment of the natural environments that RV camping offers.

# CONCLUSION

As we conclude "Escape to Nature: RV Camping Tips for National Park Enthusiasts," it's time to reflect on the journey we have embarked upon through the pages of this guide. The essence of this book has been to equip readers with the knowledge and inspiration needed to explore the natural beauty of national parks via RV camping, while also emphasizing the importance of responsible and sustainable practices.

RV camping in national parks is more than a leisure activity; it's a profound way to connect with nature and experience the diverse landscapes and ecosystems these parks protect. We've delved into the essentials of RV camping, from preparing and maintaining your vehicle to setting up a comfortable and safe campsite. Understanding the mechanics and dynamics of your RV is not just a practical necessity but also a part of the adventure, empowering you to be self-reliant and confident on your journey.

Safety has been a recurring theme in our exploration. Venturing into the wilderness carries inherent risks, and being prepared for emergencies is paramount. We've covered how to handle mechanical failures, weather-related challenges, and encounters with wildlife, stressing the importance of preparation, calm decision-making, and respect for nature's unpredictability. These guidelines are not meant to intimidate but to prepare enthusiasts for a safe and enjoyable journey.

The beauty of national parks is timeless, but it is also vulnerable. Our discussions on sustainable RV practices and minimizing our environmental impact are crucial. We've explored how adopting eco-friendly habits, such as reducing energy consumption, conserving water, managing waste effectively, and practicing Leave No Trace principles, can make a significant difference. These practices ensure that the pristine beauty of these parks is preserved for future generations to witness and enjoy.

One of the most enchanting aspects of RV camping in national parks is the opportunity to observe wildlife in its natural habitat. We've emphasized the importance of doing so responsibly. Respecting wildlife and understanding how to coexist with them safely enhances the camping experience while ensuring the well-being of these magnificent creatures.

Throughout the book, we've also focused on the personal aspects of RV camping. From fostering family bonds to finding solitary peace, the RV experience caters to diverse desires and goals. The adaptability of RV camping makes it an ideal way to explore the vastness of national parks, whether you seek adventure, relaxation, or a bit of both.

As we conclude, it's evident that RV camping in national parks is more than just a vacation option; it's a lifestyle choice that embraces the spirit of exploration and respect for the natural world. The tips and insights in this guide are designed to help enthusiasts navigate this lifestyle with confidence and environmental consciousness.

In closing, "Escape to Nature: RV Camping Tips for National Park Enthusiasts" is more than a manual; it's a call to adventure, inviting readers to embark on a journey of discovery, learning, and connection with the great outdoors. As you close this book and plan your next RV trip, remember that each journey contributes to a lifetime of memories and experiences. The national parks await with their unspoiled beauty and untold stories, ready to be explored and cherished responsibly. The road is open, the nature is calling – it's time to answer the call with enthusiasm and respect, embracing the wilderness in all its splendor.

*Thank you for buying and reading/ listening to our book. If you found this book useful/ helpful please take a few minutes and leave a review on the platform where you purchased our book. Your feedback matters greatly to us.*